✪✪✪✪✪✪✪✪✪✪✪✪✪✪✪✪✪✪

The Literature of Higher Education 1971

✪✪✪✪✪✪✪✪✪✪✪✪✪✪✪✪✪✪

Lewis B. Mayhew

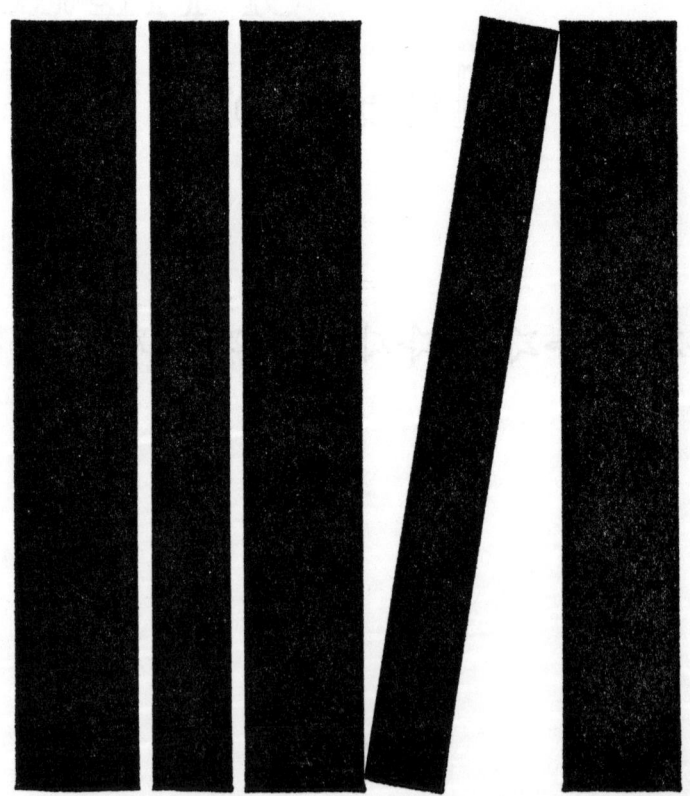

THE LITERATURE
OF
HIGHER EDUCATION
1971

 Jossey-Bass Inc., Publishers
615 Montgomery Street • San Francisco • 1971

THE LITERATURE OF HIGHER EDUCATION 1971
    Lewis B. Mayhew

**Copyright © 1971 by American Association for Higher Education
Jossey-Bass Inc., Publishers**

Copyright under Pan American and Universal Copyright
Conventions. All rights reserved. No part of this
book may be reproduced in any form—except for brief
quotation (not to exceed 1,000 words) in a review or
professional work—without permission in writing from
the publishers. Address all inquiries to:

*Jossey-Bass, Inc., Publishers
615 Montgomery Street
San Francisco, California 94111*

Library of Congress Catalog Card Number 74-155167

International Standard Book Number ISBN 0-87589-092-X

Manufactured in the United States of America
    *Composed and printed by York Composition Company, Inc.
    Bound by Chas. H. Bohn & Co., Inc.*

JACKET DESIGN BY WILLI BAUM, SAN FRANCISCO

FIRST EDITION

Code 7118

The Jossey-Bass Series in Higher Education

General Editors

JOSEPH AXELROD
*San Francisco State College
and University of California, Berkeley*

MERVIN B. FREEDMAN
*San Francisco State College
and Wright Institute, Berkeley*

PREFACE

This book on the literature of higher education has come to be an annual affair. The exercise of writing it is at the same time a labor of love, a self-imposed discipline, and a race against time. Given the complexities of higher education, those active in its operation do not have time to read the crescendoing flood of books, yet they should know the general content and quality. Thus this analysis attempts to provide enough substance so that one can know the essence without reading the book itself. It also attempts to assess and evaluate, using the highly personalized criteria I have evolved through reading most of what is published each year. As a professional student of higher education I feel I must be aware of what is being written, although I recognize that without the stimulus of a

Preface

publisher's deadline I would fail. Hence, painful though some of the reading is, it once again has been done.

This yearly effort was begun originally at the suggestion of Lawrence Dennis and appeared as an article in the *Educational Record*. It has been continued at the request of the American Association for Higher Education. In the past the book has focused on just the literature of the previous year. In this volume in the first chapter I reflect on the literature published generally since 1965 in the belief that higher education during the 1970s will be qualitatively different. In order to anticipate these changes, some retrospection is appropriate. This historical chapter was originally prepared for the ERIC Clearinghouse on Higher Education.

I do not know how long one person can continue to digest sometimes indigestible literature. Each year the task becomes larger. But I do believe that there will continue to be a need for a one-man synthesis of the literature. If this volume approximates that ideal I shall be satisfied.

Stanford, California　　　　　　　　　　　　　　　LEWIS B. MAYHEW
February 1971

CONTENTS

	Preface	ix
1	Trends in the Literature 1965-1970	1
2	Literature of 1971	32
3	Governance	35
4	History	52
5	Campus Unrest	67

Contents

6	Reflections	83
7	Institutional Differences	93
8	Conference Proceedings and Symposia	106
9	Teaching and Other Professional Procedures	115
10	Curriculum	124
11	Economic Analyses of Basic Assumptions	132
12	Briefly Reviewed	144
	Index	156

✪✪✪✪✪✪✪✪✪✪✪✪✪✪✪✪✪

The Literature
of Higher
Education 1971

✪✪✪✪✪✪✪✪✪✪✪✪✪✪✪✪✪

One

TRENDS IN THE LITERATURE 1965-1970

The literature concerning higher education has steadily increased in volume and erratically increased in quality from 1965 to 1970. Although the time lag seems to be decreasing, books and monographs generally reflected the concerns of several years before. Thus, in 1964, the year of Berkeley, only four books could be identified which dealt with students; and two of those really codified work completed even several years earlier. By 1969–1970, books dealing with students were being produced at crescendoing rates. At the beginning of the period covered by this review, relatively few books or monographs were based on systematic research, being for the most part reflections or exhortations. By 1969–70, though many polemical titles continued to emerge, a substantial number of reports with a reasonable empirical base were published. Throughout the period conference proceedings and anthologies flourished, frequently under somewhat misleading titles, which is a serious weakness. There is as yet no good way of identifying and retrieving the solid and lasting from the mass of superficial material contained in such compendia.

The periodical press reflected several different characteristics in its treatment of higher education. Professional journals, exemplified by *Liberal Education, The Educational Record, The Journal of Higher Education,* and *The Journal of General Education,* maintained a steady if somewhat too pedantic flow of revised speeches, descriptions of courses and programs, exhortative papers and occasional research-based reports. The two journals which maintained a consistently high level of style and thoughtfulness were *The Graduate Journal,* produced by the University of Texas, and *Daedalus;* both presented much of substance well worth preserving between hard covers. It is wise that at least some of the issues of *Daedalus* are being released in more permanent form. Several journals, although designed for a specialized audience, did present a number of reports of empirical studies, as did *College and University, The Journal of College Student Personnel,* and *College Board Review;* and several new journals appeared showing considerable promise although by no means restricting themselves to higher education alone—*Compact,* published by the Higher Education Commission of the States, and *Youth and Society,* published by Sage Publications in southern California. Each made important contributions. *College and University Business* and *College Management* each provided reasonably fresh and complete topical coverage, along with a great deal of advertising of interest chiefly to planning and management people and those concerned with purchasing. Another new journal with ex-

Trends in the Literature 1965–1970

cellent potential is *Change in Higher Education,* which explores through well-styled articles and essays the whole problem of innovation.

The popular periodical press reveals the greatest change in coverage of higher education. By the end of the decade such journals as *Fortune, Look,* and *Life* had each devoted single issues to collegiate problems, and *Harper's, The Atlantic, New Republic* and *Saturday Review* increased the attention given to the academy. The daily press also reflected the greater significance of higher education in the national consciousness and covered educational matters with steadily increasing sophistication. Although the primary position of the *New York Times* as a source of information has not been challenged, it has been augmented by distinguished coverage in such papers as the *Los Angeles Times, Baltimore Sun, Washington Post, Des Moines Register,* and the *Wall Street Journal.* There was a time when one could almost ignore the daily press in searching for patterns of higher education, but this is no longer true. Fully two-thirds of one major digest of higher education news which is distributed periodically to a limited audience consists of daily press reporting of essential value; the *Chronicle of Higher Education* is attempting to keep the profession immediately informed not only of national developments affecting colleges and universities but of the substance of books, reports, and conferences as they are released or happen.

A particularly productive source of information must be described as fugitive literature. This consists of both mimeograph or offset reports and well-printed, soft-cover documents distributed to a limited audience. Outstanding examples are the research reports produced by the American College Testing Program; some of the occasional reports put out by the College Entrance Examination Board, such as Warren W. Willingham's "Patterns of Admission for Transfer Students"; the monographs produced by the Institute for Higher Education at the University of Georgia or the Southeastern Junior College Leadership Center; and studies published by various universities which are not necessarily released by the university press. The University of Minnesota (1969) released "Minnesota Ph.D.s

Evaluate Their Training," the University of Massachusetts has published several thoughtful essays by its former president, John W. Lederle, and the Board of Regents for Ohio has printed a number of important statements by its chancellor, John Millett. Also under this rubric of fugitive literature must be placed the enormous volume of state studies and master plans for higher education which contain some of the most solid information now available. The California Master Plan for Higher Education, the various specialized studies of the Board of Higher Education for Illinois, and the periodic revisions of The New York State Master Plan are simply illustrative. Even more difficult to locate are institutional studies and reports, some of which are of exceptionally high quality and of general interest. The ten volumes of the Study of Education at Stanford and the long-range academic plan for Vanderbilt University exemplify some of the best of this genre.

Without really being able to know, one can surmise that the greatest volume of literature about higher education, of both high and low quality, is contained in conference proceedings of one sort or another. There are published reports of conferences conducted by individual institutions, by foundations, by centers and institutes, and of course by the various regional and national associations. Several of the more widely distributed and comprehensive are the proceedings from the college and university self-study institutes conducted jointly by the Western Interstate Commission for Higher Education and the Center for Research and Development in Higher Education at the University of California at Berkeley, the background papers and addresses given at the annual meeting of the American Council on Education, and the papers delivered at the National Conference on Higher Education conducted by the American Association for Higher Education. These are readily known and available. However, there are many other reports not as widely disseminated but of potentially equal value. For example, the Duke University Press has released *Management Information Systems in Higher Education: The State of the Art* (C. B. Johnson and W. G. Katzenmeyer, 1969), which reports the 1969 conference; and Regis

Trends in the Literature 1965–1970

College published *Guidelines for Jesuit Higher Education* (1969), which was the workshop proceedings from a 1969 meeting of Jesuit educators.

An unknown terrain, unknown simply because the dimension and quality have never been carefully assessed, are doctoral theses by students in the growing number of higher education programs. There have been a few attempts to publish annotated bibliographies of these, but for the most part they are quite specialized and sporadic. For example, several attempts have been made to publish annotations of theses dealing with junior college administration; and Indiana University has occasionally tried to catalogue theses in education. A cursory glance at just some of this literature suggests that much of it is not particularly useful for broad generalization. However, it does represent a source which should be systematically examined in the future, particularly since so many institutions are now offering work in higher education.

Neither education nor higher education has ever been particularly well served with bibliography. The Institute for Higher Education at Columbia did produce several published bibliographies, as did the College Entrance Examination Board. The American Association for Higher Education does publish commentary on both the periodical and monographic press, and the ERIC Clearinghouses are beginning to produce useful but still incomplete bibliographies. (The ERIC Clearinghouse on Higher Education, for example, has produced General Bibliographies No. 1 and 2 which appear reasonably representative of available material.) For the most part, however, one wishing to examine the field must rely on primitive forms of search and retrieval. If higher education is truly as pivotal in the national life as is claimed, this bibliographic problem should be solved and solved quickly.

Publishers of material about higher education also reflect changing patterns. At one time, Harper seemed preeminent in the field, only to be replaced by McGraw-Hill. During the period 1965–1970, several publishers emerged as the biggest producers of useful material. Praeger, Jossey-Bass, and McCutchan all made available new materials, and McGraw-Hill, as it began to publish reports

The Literature of Higher Education 1971

from the Carnegie Commission on Higher Education and to expand its long-existing series in higher education, reestablished the position it held in the late 1950s. Among the non-commercial publishers, the American Council on Education and the Southern Regional Education Board were principal sources.

Anyone attempting to classify the literature of the complex phenomenon which is American higher education would develop his own categories; hence this analysis of trends must be viewed as somewhat idiosyncratic. With that caveat, there seem to be at least eleven major trends or strands which are reasonably well documented over the past five years. People working in higher education seem extraordinarily introspective about the nature of their enterprise and considerable literature interprets the essential qualities of collegiate education. This is by no means a new phenomenon and the classics of earlier ages, such as Newman and Veblen, are still germane. However, in recent times, authors have struggled over such issues as whether the university was a servant of society or a self-regenerating critic and instructor of society; whether the university was primarily a servant, a place for the production or dissemination of knowledge, or some combination of these; whether the university had emerged as a pivotal institution in the society or still remained only one of a number of social institutions of somewhat equal social utility. The more significant literature elaborating such questions is found in book form or in essays contained in journals of general opinion. Clark Kerr really initiated the present phase with the publication of his *The Uses of the University* (Harvard University Press, 1963), in which he saw institutions of higher education developing almost without guidance into complex multipurpose establishments designed to provide a variety of services. Then others took up the investigation. Jacques Barzun, *The American University* (Harper and Row, 1968), believes that a collegiate institution is a unique and self-renewing entity which has been jeopardized as institutions have attempted to provide services for which they were ill-equipped. Harold Taylor, *Students Without Teachers: the Crisis in the University* (McGraw-Hill, 1969), feels that the university can only restore itself when it becomes an active agent in recreating a

Trends in the Literature 1965–1970

society gone wrong. Generally, discussions of the nature of the university in 1965 assumed a primary role, for higher education was being challenged by militant students and by politically oriented restrictions on finance. By 1970, writers were at least willing to recognize that education and higher education had to compete with other social needs such as renovation of cities, rectification of a polluted atmosphere, or refurbishing an obsolete and inadequate public health effort. Perhaps the tone of commentary was best captured in an editorial in *Change* magazine, "The End of the Bull Market" (January-February 1970). Especially in the last half of the period under review there emerged the beginnings of an examination of the university's relationship with the urban condition. Editorial writers called for urban grant institutions. Conference proceedings urged the university to help solve pressing urban problems, and descriptive literature enumerated the creation or the will to create university-based centers for urban studies. However, even this visible problem was treated differently: some writers claimed that the university would destroy itself if it used its resources for such quixotic undertakings while others saw the university as the last hope. A related strand which reached its peak in 1969 was the debate over the proper posture for colleges and universities to take regarding the war in Vietnam. Earlier literature assumed that it was quite proper for the university to support the government in its foreign policy and to help out by lending expertise to research needs, even if these did involve military operation. However, a questioning attitude developed, sparked to a large extent by the efforts of dissenting and protesting students; and statements began to appear suggesting that the university should get out of such things as defense-based research, offering ROTC work or allowing military recruiters to come onto campuses. Little concerning this topic is found in the professional periodical press but a great deal in the daily press by means of reports of speeches, teach-ins, and actual confrontations on the campus. The issue is even more thoroughly aired in the burgeoning number of reports and explanations of such events as the crisis at Columbia. Student writers and their apologists seem generally persuaded that higher education should divorce itself from national military and political policy. However, by late 1969, several books, such as those by Sidney Hook, Charles Frankel, and George Kennan, began to refute student arguments.

One essential matter which had received virtually no serious attention before 1965, with the exception of that given by conservative economists such as Roger Freeman, was the question of who benefits from higher education and who pays. Prior to 1965, conventional wisdom held that society in the long run gained most from a well-developed system of higher education, hence the public should pay the largest proportion of the cost. This was the period of increasing fellowship, scholarship and loan provisions, and strident argument against tuition increases in public institutions. By late 1969 and early 1970, however, news releases, a number of speeches, quite a few journal articles, and several commission reports began to urge that ultimately it was the individual himself who gained most from attending college, and it was the individual himself who should be expected to pay the heaviest burden for the advantages sure to accrue to him. So pronounced was this shift that in the spring of 1970 Howard Bowen was virtually the only economist who could be found to espouse publicly the older dogma.

With so much introspection about the nature of collegiate institutions, it is remarkable that so few historical interpretations have emerged recently. The last of major consequence was Laurence R. Veysey's *The Emergence of the American University* (University of Chicago Press, 1970), which provides historical support for a belief in the centrality of colleges and universities in the American life. That thesis is supported by another major work which while not essentially historical makes considerable use of historical materials and trends. That book, of course, is Christopher Jencks and David Riesman, *The Academic Revolution* (Doubleday, 1968).

The second major topic is concerned with collegiate organization, administration, and governance, and is exemplified by reasonably comprehensive treatment given to a number of subcategories. The presidency, which earlier had been described in a number of reminiscences or impressionistic studies, received almost apocalyptic treatment during the period 1965–1970. The daily press

Trends in the Literature 1965–1970

dwelt on the high incidence of presidential resignations, and both the popular and professional periodical press emphasized the impossibility of the president's task given the enormity of changes in higher education. The student outbreaks at both Cornell and Columbia were occasions for elaborate editorializing, and the suggestion by Yale president Kingman Brewster, Jr., that presidents' conduct of office should be reviewed periodically, sparked another sustained sequence of writings. No major book dealing exclusively with the college presidency appeared, and only a few argued for restoration of considerable power to the college president so that he might govern. J. Douglas Brown, in *The Liberal University* (McGraw-Hill, 1969), was one of those who felt there had been excessive erosion of presidential prerogatives.

Attracting considerably more attention was the matter of faculty organization and faculty participation in collegiate governance. One of the earlier reports was that of a task force commissioned by the American Association for Higher Education which urged shared responsibility and a senate-style of governance as being the only appropriate way to conduct collegiate business. Following that came considerable argument in the professional press and in conference proceedings about which was preferable: some form of shared responsibility or adversary-style governance through unionism. Most of the major national organizational conferences devoted at least one annual meeting to this matter and their proceedings present collectively most of the known argument and information about the subject. Several universities conducted intensive studies of their own systems of governance and a few allowed these to be published and distributed nationally. An outstanding example is that by Caleb Foote and others, *The Culture of the University: Governance and Education* (Jossey-Bass, 1968), which is a blueprint for the University of California at Berkeley.

In spite of an actual proliferation of administrative subspecialties, literature describing the duties and characteristics needed is relatively sparse. Arthur Dibden did prepare an anthology on *Academic Deanship in American Colleges and Universities* (Southern Illinois University Press, 1968), and Paul L. Dressel has several articles dealing with the academic department which by implication treat department heads. And several of the specialized journals do discuss the role of admissions counselor, business manager and financial aids officer. Several articles have dealt with the new concept of ombudsman, and a few have dealt tangentially with the role of development officer. However, as compared with the 1930s, when a rather comprehensive literature about academic deans appeared, or the 1950s, when much was written about counselors and deans of students, the present period has not been productive. During the first half of the decade of the sixties, considerable was written about directors of institutional research, but apparently it is assumed that this role is now sufficiently delimited; current articles dealing with institutional research concentrate more on the actual problems to be solved. A similar flourishing of literature about long-range planners has thus far not been developed. However, a number of the centers for higher education have published workshop or conference proceedings which do delineate some of the duties of administrative sub-specialties; and the annual conference on academic deans held each year in Oklahoma publishes proceedings regularly. The Institute for Higher Education of the University of Georgia has probably produced the most materials concerning academic administrative officers.

Collegiate finance is much in the news, much in polemical writing, but is not as well covered by scholarly publications as might be expected, given the crisis nature of the period 1965–70. Generally, the literature reveals the serious financial plight of private institutions, and several of the alumni publications of institutions such as Princeton describe in detail the exact amount of anticipated deficits. Also, there has been a good bit written about the contributions the states have made to public higher education during the decade of the sixties, and how much more will be needed during the seventies. The publications of several national study groups, for example the Carnegie Commission on Higher Education, have explored various alternatives by which federal support can be provided institutions, and each of the three regional compacts (Southern Regional Education Board, the New England Board of Higher Edu-

Trends in the Literature 1965–1970

cation, and Western Interstate Commission on Higher Education) has published material stressing both the economic need and contribution of higher education; but no major treatise such as Seymour Harris' *Higher Education: Resources and Finance* (McGraw-Hill, 1962) has recently appeared. However, reports of several states investigating whether or not public aid should or could be furnished private higher education have appeared, and a cluster of other states are conducting such inquiries with the expectation that reports will be issued. A peripheral matter, which could be considered under any of several headings, did receive a good bit of daily press coverage in the last part of 1969. This was the financial implications of student protest and demonstration. Articles described drops in alumni giving, failures of bond elections and increased insurance cost because of student outrages. As yet no careful study and reporting has been completed.

An enormous volume of material has appeared dealing with the problems and issues of statewide coordination, long-range planning and control. This subject received its first attention in 1957 with the publication of *The Efficiency of Freedom* (Johns Hopkins University Press) and Lyman A. Glenny's *The Autonomy of Public Colleges* (McGraw-Hill, 1959). But in the last half of the 1960s, almost every state completed a state study of higher education, or developed a master plan, or developed elaborate sets of recommendations, and these have been widely disseminated, at least within the states themselves. The problems of long-range planning and control have received some conference attention with resulting publication. However, it was not until 1970 that five major research reports concerned with statewide coordination and control were finally made public. The general tenor of the literature on this subject is that voluntary systems of coordination have proven ineffective and that some form of mandatory coordination and control is probably essential; there is a strong likelihood that statewide boards of control are the next logical step. Within the private sector there has developed a great deal of interest in consortia and clustering of groups of private institutions for mutual benefit; and information regarding these is gradually creeping into the literature. An especially informative though fugitive example is *The Acquainter,* which disseminates news of consortia. Within the professional journals, however, is a strong sampling of articles describing how such things as the Great Lakes College Association are actually faring.

Boards of trustees have received some attention. Several major studies describing the characteristics of board members were completed in 1969. Boards and board members have also received a great deal of daily press coverage as a result of charges that they were unresponsive to present generations of college students. A few articles appeared tracing the origin of boards of trustees, and several manuals for the guidance of new board members were developed. A major issue brought into focus is whether the lay board of trustees is anachronistic. Gerald P. Burns in *Trustees in Higher Education* (Independent College Funds of America, 1966) firmly believes that they are not. However, radical student writings argue for the abolition of boards accompanied by a devolution of real responsibility to students and faculty. A few conference papers and the several research reports on statewide systems have tried to analyze the relationship between institutional boards of trustees and more complex systems, but no even quasi-definitive study has been reported.

Reflecting a potentially profound change in higher education governance is the growing body of discussion on the pros and cons of unionism. Several states have legislated collective bargaining for public colleges and universities, and these acts have been accompanied by considerable editorializing and news coverage. At least three books have appeared during the past five years dealing with unionism and collective bargaining, and three or four conference proceedings have presented papers, either analytical or polemical. Several articles in the *AAUP Bulletin* have evidenced a shift in attitude toward collective bargaining and the strike, and the previously mentioned AAHE study of governance examines unionism as one option for at least underdeveloped institutions. A few articles describe the peculiar affinity of junior college faculty members for unionism, and the prediction has been made that if unionism ever does succeed in higher education, it will enjoy its first and greatest growth within junior colleges and former state teachers colleges.

Trends in the Literature 1965–1970

Increasingly, collegiate institutions are forced to deal with the courts, and this has occasioned greater coverage in the literature. While there have been no books dealing with college law which are similar to an earlier one written by Thomas Blackwell, there have been several summaries of court decisions, notably the one periodically prepared by M. M. Chambers. Robert Funk summarized proscriptive legislation in the October 1970 issue of *Compact,* and the American Personnel and Guidance Association released a monograph analyzing court decisions affecting student personnel work. Within periodical literature, the focus for the past several years has been the relationship of colleges to the courts. Now that the *in loco parentis* doctrine is almost dead, some have feared that increasing recourse to due process procedures in the courts would be destructive of the autonomy of an institution. James Perkins, for example, has written eloquently on this subject; but others, such as Clark Byse of the Harvard Law School, have written several papers approving of greater use of due process. From mid-1969 on, there was a flurry of articles dealing with the use of injunction as a way of controlling student protest, and there has been at least one summary released by the American Council on Education pointing out potentialities and dangers of the injunction. *College and University Business* regularly publishes a small column analyzing recent court decisions, and a few recent court cases, such as those dealing with accreditation for Parsons College or for a proprietary school, have received some coverage.

For years collegiate institutions were conducted with very little long-range planning. However, in the year 1960 it became apparent that planning was essential, given the rapid expansion of higher education. This awareness has produced a volume of literature which contrasts markedly with Sidney Tickton's solitary effort in the mid-1950s. There have been four or five books which tried to explain the potential uses of program planning and budgeting, or cost benefit analysis for institutions of higher education. Four or five conferences have been devoted to the subject and proceedings released, and there have been several didactic articles in the professional press, urging greater attention to long-range planning. Each

The Literature of Higher Education 1971

one of the state master plans instructs individual campuses to prepare their own plans and a few of these have been discussed in article form. Related has been the growing literature concerning uses of the computer in planning and management. The examples range from Bushnell and Allen, *The Computer in American Education* (Wiley, 1967), which is a conference proceeding, to the small book written for the layman and released by The American Council on Education on how the computer could be used. There has been only one serious negative note regarding long-range planning, and that is M. M. Chambers' *Freedom and Repression in Higher Education* (Bloomcraft, 1965). Actually, Chambers is not so much concerned about planning as he is about the implications for control which planning threatens. *College and University Business* and *College Management* have each contributed much anecdotal material to the literature on planning, but nowhere does one find a comprehensive manual on planning which can help individual institutions accomplish it.

Beginning in approximately 1958, college faculty members became more and more concerned about salaries and fringe benefits as they realized that relative to other segments of the population they had actually lost in real wages steadily since the end of World War II, and this concern is again reflected by literature. The *AAUP Bulletin* produces its report card on salaries paid by different institutions, and the NEA Research Division develops similar norms. Mark Ingram prepared *The Outward Fringe* (University of Wisconsin, 1965), which deals with faculty benefits, and *The Mirror of Brass* (University of Wisconsin Press, 1968), which deals with compensation for administrators. Within the professional press are to be found discussions of the relative worth of increasing salaries or increasing fringe benefits. Particularly in 1965–1967, a few articles appeared discussing the professoriate as an affluent group. In the daily press considerable space has been given to efforts by this, that or the other state to maintain faculty salaries at a level competitive with other states.

In view of the proclaimed significance of academic freedom to the functioning of American colleges and universities, this subject

Trends in the Literature 1965–1970

has received surprisingly little attention in any systematic way. The *AAUP Handbook on Academic Freedom and Tenure* (University of Wisconsin Press, 1967) presents some of the basic documents. Walter Metzger and others have prepared a small book of essays on academic freedom, and the *AAUP Journal* presents its investigated cases of breaches of academic freedom. Charles Frankel in *Education and the Barricades* (Norton, 1969) and T. R. McConnell in a series of essays have suggested some limitation on academic freedom by emphasizing professorial responsibilities. One book and several doctoral theses have pondered the threat to academic freedom from loyalty oaths. A growing body of editorial comment in the daily press urges that tenure is no longer needed and indeed is serving as a detriment to institutional operations. Some of the protest literature contends that student academic freedom has been consistently violated and makes the accompanying demand that students be freed from virtually all regulation. There have been only a few suggestions that academic freedom as presently codified might be obsolete; but several conference proceedings in 1969 and 1970 began to raise that issue.

Whereas before 1964 the literature concerning college students was erratic in both quality and frequency of appearance and not particularly revealing of what students were like, since 1965 there has been a torrent of writing in all media. National conferences devoted full plenary sessions to students and published the proceedings. The popular and professional press issued think-piece after think-piece trying to interpret the generational conflict. The daily press seemed to give even greater attention to college students as college students than it previously did to intercollegiate athletics. Most of the publishers issuing works on higher education brought out several titles dealing with students, and the various research installations such as the American College Testing Program or the Center for Research and Development in Higher Education at Berkeley produced impressive studies of student characteristics, student ability, student success in college and modes of student development through the college years. The volume has been so great and the content so varied that no definitive classification by subject is as yet possible. However, several distinct threads are perceptible. First, there have been numerous attempts to portray student characteristics—research monographs from the American College Testing Program, several monographs authored by Alexander Astin from data obtained by the American Council on Education, studies conducted by the several centers for the study of higher education. To these largely quantitative reports must be added more qualitative descriptions, exemplified by Kenneth Keniston's books on *The Uncommitted* (Harcourt Brace Jovanovich, 1965) and *The Young Radicals* (Harcourt Brace Jovanovich, 1968), together with his substantial contribution to the popular and semiprofessional press. There have also been numerous attempts to characterize special categories of students. For example, Lawrence A. Pervin and others describe *The College Dropout and the Utilization of Talent* (Princeton University Press, 1966), Paul Heist (ed.) presents *The Creative College Student* (Jossey-Bass, 1968) and the American College Testing Program reports on *The Two-Year College and Its Students* (1970).

Then, of course, student dissent, protest and violence have seemingly attracted the attention of virtually every well-known author about higher education as well as a substantial number of the student protesting group itself. This literature exists on a continuum from that highly favorable to youth, such as Otto Butz' *To Make a Difference* (Harper and Row, 1967), to the angry historical and psychoanalytic interpretation by Lewis Feuer in *The Conflict of Generations* (Basic Books, 1969). In the popular press, Harold Taylor has contributed several essays praising student revolutionaries, while George Kennan takes youth to task for irresponsibility. The daily press for the most part seems editorially biased against student outbreaks; but careful scrutiny of daily coverage provides an overall basis for inference. Then, too, the students themselves have contributed much, beginning with published essays by Mario Savio, Paul Potter, and Tom Hayden, interpreting the Berkeley crisis, to the more recently written *The Strawberry Statement* (James S. Kunen, Random House, 1969) and the more pedestrian *Police on Campus* (New York Civil Liberties Union, 1969). The

Trends in the Literature 1965–1970

worldwide nature of student revolt has not gone unnoticed. A number of articles appearing in the popular press compare student protest nation-to-nation. Then several monographs have appeared, such as Raymond Aron's *The Elusive Revolution* (Praeger, 1969), which compares French with American student protest, or Donald K. Emmerson's *Students and Politics in Developing Nations* (Praeger, 1968). There is at least one student-produced crosscultural analysis, written by Barbara and John Ehrenreich, *Long March, Short Spring* (Monthly Review, 1969).

A related literature deals with student uses and abuses of sex, drugs, and search for new experiences. The literature on sex provides a wide spectrum of views. Gael Greene asserts that there has been a major sexual revolution and that promiscuity is the order of the day on college campuses, while the calmer analyses of Joseph Katz or Mervin Freedman argue that the real sexual revolution took place in the 1920s and that contemporary college sexuality is really a constrained matter more expressive of search for companionship or identity than for pure sexuality. However, the word "sex" still seems to have a magical appeal—the daily press is constantly on the alert to report articles or papers discussing student sex behavior. While sexuality is discussed in a number of monographs focusing on college students, there have been relatively few monographic or book-length treatments of the subject per se. Nor have conference proceedings devoted much attention to this matter. Second only to sex is the literature dealing with student use of drugs, and what is generally available either assumes or seeks to establish that there is widespread use of drugs on the campus. Beyond doubt, the best single treatment of this tense subject is Helen H. Nowlis' *Drugs on the College Campus* (Anchor, 1968), or the two-volume quantitative report presented by the Blums and published by Jossey-Bass (Richard H. Blum & Associates, *Society and Drugs; Students and Drugs,* 1969). Then there are several works which deal with local drug conditions, as does James T. Carey in *The College Drug Scene* (Prentice-Hall, 1968), which delves in detail into the dynamics of the Berkeley drug colony. The third element of this cluster involves student search for new experience, and this is provided a reasonable but less com-

The Literature of Higher Education 1971

prehensive coverage. Within the professional journals, the significance of sensitivity training and of student interest in the arts and in small group activities is described and analyzed, while in the popular press such phenomena as rock concerts and nude parties received some attention. This particular aspect has received considerable attention from campus ministers and theologians who attempt to interpret the student quest for new experience in theological terms. Father Andrew Greeley's brilliant essay on "The Psychedelic and the Sacred" (in G. Kerry Smith, ed., *Agony and Promise,* Jossey-Bass, 1969) and the book-length treatment by Donald L. Rogan entitled *Campus Apocalypse* (Seabury, 1969) are examples. Some writing concerning curricular matters deals with the search for new experience but does so tangentially, as in the numerous pleas for great availability of opportunity for actual experience in the performing and creative arts.

A perplexing question for students and practitioners has been: "What is the overall impact of colleges on students?" In the mid-1950s the first book in what was to become an expanding literature appeared, Phillip Jacob's *Changing Values in College* (Harper and Row, 1957). Since that time, in the professional press and in monographic and conference literature, there have been literally thousands of attempts to answer the question. Much of this literature is summarized by Kenneth A. Feldman and Theodore M. Newcomb in their two-volume work on *The Impact of College on Students* (Jossey-Bass, 1969). This really brings the story up to date following Nevitt Sanford's earlier compendium, *The American College* (Wiley, 1962). However, special attention should be called to various report theories issued by the paraeducational organizations such as the testing agencies which present data only recently made possible through the use of high-speed computers. The overall burden of this literature is that college students do change, frequently in ways thought to be desirable, but that the relationship of that change to what colleges and universities actually do is far from clear. Alexander Astin, for example, showed that the impact of the highly selective prestige institution was far from significant. This material on the impact of college on students

Trends in the Literature 1965-1970

has of course been used by many critics and polemicists who write on the subject of higher education. Hence there is a substantial body of secondary interpretation containing considerable clinical insight to go with the primary data in the research reports themselves.

Curriculum and instruction, although frequently presumed to be central in higher education, seem to have received quantitatively less attention in any medium than such things as student protest or the nature of collegiate education, and college teaching itself is but sparsely treated. It is true that one journal, *Improving College and University Teaching,* concentrates on technique and that several other journals, notably the *AAJC Journal,* contain resumés of successful teaching. Nevertheless, other subjects more frequently engaged the attention of writers. Wilbert J. McKeachie does produce a reasonably steady stream of material, and James W. Thornton and James Brown have produced a useful handbook on teaching; but for the most part college teaching has not been systematically examined or reported upon in research literature. A few conference proceedings have focused on teaching and several collections of papers have dealt with innovation in teaching. Within the popular and periodical press the phenomenon which John Gardner labeled as "the flight from teaching" has been discussed, as well as—especially in the daily press and in editorials—the subject of "publish or perish" and the relationship of teaching to research.

The undergraduate curriculum is a hardy perennial in the professional press. The articles frequently extol the values of the liberal arts but rarely suggest to the practitioner how the various liberal arts and sciences can be put together. Those journals also contain a heavy sprinkling of descriptions of new course organization; the most frequently cited changes involve some rearrangement of the academic calendar and some entry into interdisciplinary work. General education, which during the 1950s attracted more attention than any other curricular matter, received considerably less attention in the late sixties, except at several conferences and in Daniel Bell's *Reforming of General Education* (Columbia University Press, 1966). Much more publicized were various attempts to make undergraduate curricula more flexible and more relevant through articles dealing with free university-style courses, ad hoc courses, and greater attention to independent study. The educational significance of how students are grouped also received fair coverage in both articles and monographs, with some variant of the cluster college idea being the most frequently treated. As compared with other five-year periods in the recent past, 1965–1970 saw a larger number of book-length treatments of curricular theory. Paul L. Dressel's *College and University Curriculum* (McCutchan, 1968), Lewis B. Mayhew's *Contemporary College Students and the Curriculum* (Southern Regional Education Board, 1969), Joseph Schwab's *College Curriculum and Student Protest* (University of Chicago Press, 1969), and Joseph Tussman's *Experiment at Berkeley* (Oxford University Press, 1969) are simply examples of this expanding body of literature.

For some time prior to 1965, the general literature concerning higher education contained little specifically germane to professional education. However, since the mid-part of the decade there have been an increasing number of monographs, articles, anthologies and commission reports dealing with professional education, the needs and direction of change. The National Society for Engineering Education has over the years published a wide range of articles dealing with the relationship between general and engineering education, and the relationship between engineering science and applied engineering subjects. Organizations concerned with business administration, such as the American Association of Schools of Business, have begun to devote more attention to specifically curricular issues, and some of the schools of business themselves have arranged for conferences and published proceedings containing much curricular content. Since 1965, there have been several national symposia on legal and medical education, and these contain important information concerning curricular reform. Two outstanding examples are David Haber and Julius Cohen, *The Law School of Tomorrow* (Rutgers University Press, 1968), and John H. Knowles, *Views of Medical Education and Medical Care* (Harvard University Press, 1968). Nursing educators have long been interested in curricular structure and curricular improvement, and *Nursing Outlook* presents a substantial quantity of such writing. As a part of this litera-

Trends in the Literature 1965–1970

ture on professional education, *Education and World Affairs* has published a series of monographs each discussing two professions and indicating how international education was or could be woven into the curricular fabric. A major summary of that effort is contained in a single volume entitled *The Professional School and World Affairs* (T. K. Glennan and others, ed., University of New Mexico Press, 1968). The American Association of Junior Colleges *Journal* has stressed technical and vocational education and contains many articles describing many programs. In addition, the several centers for the preparation of junior college administrators and teachers, such as that located in the School of Education at the University of Michigan, have also produced a reasonably steady stream of information about technical education. The more general professional journals, such as the *Journal for Higher Education* or *The Educational Record,* however, have not given the subject similar treatment. Nor has the popular periodical press or the daily press, except in the last part of 1969 and the early part of 1970, when the daily press gave some coverage to the interest of the Nixon administration in technical vocational education as a means of aiding disadvantaged groups.

International education has been the focus for a great deal of writing in many different media. Monographic treatment includes such works as David G. Scanlon et al., *Problems and Prospects in International Education* (Teachers College, Columbia, 1968), and Albert E. Gollin, *Education for National Development* (Praeger, 1970), with a broader, more interpretative overview provided by Philip H. Coombs' *The World Educational Crisis* (Oxford University Press, 1968). Within the professional periodical literature, there are a reasonable number of articles dealing with overseas campuses, centers for area studies, and the problems of bringing foreign students to American campuses and sending American students abroad for some sort of educational or research or service experience. *Education for World Affairs* turns out a steady flow of pamphlets, reports, and monographs, and one gets the impression that this organization is one of the most prolific producers. The popular press does not seem to give quite such attention to the international aspects of education, partly, one suspects, because of the greater dramatic appeal of essays interpreting student protest and dissent within the United States. At one time UNESCO published many reports dealing with international education which circulated freely within the United States; but for the past three or four years, either there has been a restriction on publishing or the results are not being widely publicized in the United States.

In view of the generally accepted notion that American higher education is becoming increasingly secular, it is rather a paradox to discover how much is currently being published having a religious or theological content. First, several books deal with issues and problems in seminary education. Then, as previously indicated, there is a persistent search to find theological meaning in some of the current activities of the young. In addition, such documents as Harry E. Smith's *Secularization and the University* (John Knox, 1968) and George N. Shuster's *Catholic Education in a Changing World* (Holt, Rinehart, and Winston, 1968) seek to elaborate a different but still vital role for the church in collegiate education. Journals such as *Motive* or the *Journal* month after month present articles of significance for both churchmen and those concerned with collegiate education. The several reports from the Danforth Foundation study of the campus ministry have added an important quantitative element to the literature, and younger scholars such as Robert Hassenger or Father Andrew M. Greeley have contributed significant studies in the tradition of the earlier critical work of Father John Tracey Ellis.

Because of student pleas for more relevant education, and because of rather pervasive criticism of the processes of education, one would expect a rather rich literature dealing with innovation and experimentation, and it is true that there are descriptions of a number of attempted changes. However, the volume and particularly the evaluative content of these materials is less than could be hoped for. Several books deal with experimentation. For example, Samuel Baskin edited *Higher Education: Some Newer Developments* (McGraw-Hill, 1965), which was a status report on experimentation up to 1965. B. Lamar Johnson in *Islands of Innovation*

Trends in the Literature 1965–1970

Expanding (Glencoe, 1969) discusses some experimentation in junior colleges, and there was one major report studying how innovations are received or rejected in a complex collegiate institution. The professional journal literature describes a number of programs which could be roughly classified under a relatively few headings. There are attempts to rearrange the academic calendar, to modify the ways in which students are grouped, to develop interdisciplinary courses, to utilize newer media, to provide off-campus experiences for students, to make the curriculum more flexible using such approaches as independent study, and to pay some attention to students' affect or impulse lives. During the period under review, a half-dozen major conferences have focused on innovation and experimentation, and the proceedings from at least a few of the important conferences have also tried to portray the state of the art. The popular press reveals little coverage, except of the more dramatic attempts to utilize sensitivity training or to develop uniquely styled cluster colleges. Innovations are apt to be merely described rather than discussed or questioned. As to which institutions will attempt innovation, Warren B. Martin has analyzed a selected sample and published the results in *Conformity* (Jossey-Bass, 1969), and JB Lon Hefferlin has discussed in *Dynamics of Academic Reform* (Jossey-Bass, 1969) the institutional factors conducive to innovation or lack of it.

One particular kind of innovation deserves specific comment—the attempt to develop interdisciplinary courses, or problem-centered courses, or courses dealing with subjects of immediate concern to students. In much of the polemical literature there are pleas for interdisciplinary work, and the journal literature contains descriptions of some of these sorts of courses, but overall there is very little discussion of how the courses fared after four or five years. One part of this interdisciplinary effort centers on courses or programs in black studies. By far the widest coverage for black studies courses has been in the daily press where they are described as responses of an embattled institution. A few of the pros and cons are contained in the professional periodical press and still more in some of the anthologies, such as James McEvoy and Abraham Miller, *Black Power and Student Rebellion* (Wadsworth, 1969). There have been at least two scholarly attempts to analyze the problems of black studies. The first of these is the book by Armstead L. Robinson and others entitled *Black Studies in the University* (Yale University Press, 1969), which presents results of an intensive seminar at Yale University, while the other is *The Black College* (Praeger, 1969) by Tilden J. LeMelle and Wilbert J. LeMelle. Beyond doubt, the issue of black studies will be increasingly important and within several years will find greater representation in the published material. The potential significance of the subject is also revealed by the fact that both the American Council on Education and the American Association for Higher Education devoted considerable portions of recent conferences to the problem of black studies and the black curriculum.

In both the 1950s and the late 1960s, colleges and universities initiated a flurry of institutional self-studies to chart curricular guidelines for the future. A number of those in the fifties were supported by the Ford Foundation and their published reports contributed to the literature of general education. During the late 1960s, institutions conducted their self-studies themselves, with the exception of some developing institutions which had outside funding for the purpose. Results of these self-studies rarely are found off the campus on which they center, but a few, such as the Study of Education at Stanford and the self-study of Oklahoma State University, have been published and distributed rather widely. Institutional self-studies are seldom treated in the periodical literature, but they do constitute an important source of information about the curriculum and hence must be considered as a discrete bibliographic category.

One last curricular element should be mentioned. This is graduate education. In an earlier period it was the subject of several important books, such as the one by Bernard Berelson, *Graduate Education in the United States* (McGraw-Hill, 1960). For the period of the review, Everett Walters' edited volume *Graduate Education Today* (American Council on Education, 1965) presents in broad outline the nature of graduate education; and several of the disciplines themselves have produced monographs indicating the state of graduate curricula and the directions in which they might evolve. Notable among these disciplines are chemistry, physics and the social and behavioral sciences. In the periodical literature, most of what one finds is critical and polemical in character; people feel that somehow something is wrong with the training provided graduate students, but few articles advance particular new solutions. The popular press and several sponsored research studies have dealt with the creation of new teaching degrees. Alden Dunham's study of state colleges conducted for the Carnegie Commission on Higher Education is the most recent and probably the most carefully done. A few dissertations have dealt with the satisfaction or dissatisfaction of graduate students with their educational experience, and several monographs have pondered the problem of excessive time imposed on students to complete the doctorate. The state of the actual graduate curricula in many different institutions is described in several guides, one being the American Council on Education's *A Guide to Graduate Study—Programs Leading to the Ph.D.* (Robert Quick, ed., 1969) and another the *Annual Guides to Graduate Study* (Karen C. Hegener, ed., Petersons Guides).

Judged only by the content of the literature of higher education, programs of colleges and universities are eclectic affairs, rooted in no particular psychological-sociological or philosophic set of presuppositions. In the 1950s, Harold Taylor did seek to categorize philosophies of higher education into the three major groups of instrumentalism, neo-humanism, and rationalism. While it is possible to force contemporary critiques of higher education into one of these three (Hutchins—rationalism, Sanford—instrumentalism), not much writing can be found reflecting a serious, systematic effort to develop a philosophic position for higher education. Thomas F. Green of Syracuse and Henry David Aiken of Brandeis have written a few essays systematically philosophical in intent. Several editors, for example Walter J. Ong in *Knowledge and the Future of Man* (Holt, Rinehart, and Winston, 1968) and RobertUlich in *Education and the Idea of Mankind* (Harcourt Brace Jovanovich, 1964), have created anthologies of material philosophical in character. For the most part, those few philosophers writing about higher education use the medium of polemical or critical essays rather than systematic analyses. Thus Charles Frankel, Sidney Hook, and Harold Taylor are better known for their popular essays than for attempts to establish systematically the parameters of a philosophy of higher education. Similarly, with the possible exception of Erik H. Erikson, who provides a psychological theory underlying the educational ideas of such writers as Arthur W. Chickering in *Education and Identity* (Jossey-Bass, 1969) and Joseph Katz & Associates in *No Time for Youth* (Jossey-Bass, 1968), there does not appear in the monographic or professional literature psychological writing appropriate for fundamental theoretical construction. Richard I. Evans has tried to derive implications from a few theorists through his published interviews, such as *Dialogue with Erik Erikson* (Harper & Row, 1967) or *B. F. Skinner: The Man and His Ideas* (Dutton, 1968); but for the most part the literature of higher education proceeds without particular reference to any psychological theory. Conference proceedings and the popular press are almost devoid of theoretical statements; and of course the daily press only occasionally refers to works of theoreticians or experimenters. While a number of the more specialized professional journals do publish reports of experimentation with different styles of teaching and different ways of organizing courses, the volume is not great nor do the results systematically support any particular approach to education. Only the work of Wilbert J. McKeachie has in the aggregate led to a reasonably stable view of teaching. A similarly bleak picture is revealed through a search for sociological bases for education. Burton Clark and Wilber Brookover have from time to time contributed to the literature, but no sociological work comparable in comprehensiveness to that of Willard Waller appeared during the late 1960s. Once again some sociologists wrote about higher education—for example, Daniel Bell in *The Reforming of General Education* (Columbia University Press, 1966) and in *Confrontation* (Daniel Bell, Irving Kristol, eds., Basic Books, 1969) and Immanuel Wallerstein in *University in Turmoil* (Atheneum, 1969)—but these are reflective critiques which are not based on any substantial amount of systematic research or theoretical formulation.

Trends in the Literature 1965–1970

A small but frequently revealing body of literature consists of novels and fiction focusing on higher education. Although no novels appeared during the 1960s which will likely last as enduring interpretations, works do reveal in caricature salient elements of collegiate education. Thus *No Transfer* (Stephen Walton, Vanguard, 1966) points to the rootlessness of competition for achievement; *The Harrad Experiment* (Robert Rimmer, Bantam, 1966) points to one utopian direction for reform; and *The Group* (Mary McCarthy, New American Library, 1965) reveals both the strengths and the decided weaknesses of higher education.

As colleges and universities have grown in size and attracted a greater variety of students, they have created a number of services which are described and analyzed in the literature of higher education. College housing has been well treated in publications of the Educational Facilities Laboratory, Inc., in several of the management-type magazines, and in the writings of directors of housing, such as Harold Riker at the University of Florida. Some of the services normally listed under student personnel work have also received adequate treatment. The student personnel series published by the American Personnel and Guidance Association treats such topics as *College Health Services in the United States* and *Faculty Advising in Colleges and Universities*. E. G. Williamson has almost singlehandedly created a bibliography on college counseling and guidance; Max Siegel in *The Counseling of College Students* (Free Press, 1968) has codified conventional wisdom; and Herbert Stroup has tried to develop a coherent view in *Toward a Philosophy of Organized Student Activities* (University of Minnesota Press, 1964). Conference proceedings and those professional journals designed specifically for student personnel workers are a richer source of information than the more general professional press or the popular periodical press. College unions have received considerable attention, largely through publications of the Association of College Unions. The College Entrance Examination Board and the American College Testing Program have produced much on the admissions process and the granting of financial aids; and the American Council on Education has provided essential service in its two guides, *American Universities and Colleges* (O. A. Singletary, ed., 1968) and *American Junior Colleges* (E. J. Gleazer, Jr., ed., 1967). Libraries and library services are not well represented among the general literature of higher education. However, one has the impression that there is a reasonably rich literature aimed at professional librarians themselves. The creation of a new journal called *The Library College* may be indicative of increased rapprochement between librarian and academician. Similarly, intercollegiate athletics and intramural athletics appear, for the most part, to be treated in rather specialized journals, with the obvious exception, of course, of the heavy coverage of intercollegiate athletics accomplished by the daily press.

As science- and university-based research have begun to encounter less than enthusiasm on the part of funding agencies, the literature rationalizing science policy and research has crescendoed. In the daily press, for example in the *Wall Street Journal*, in the popular press such as *Saturday Review*, in the popular professional press, such as *Science*, and in the professional press are found many articles seeking to justify continued heavy expenditure for research. Professional organizations such as the American Council on Education have published critiques of sponsored research, as in Stephen Strickland's *Sponsored Research in American Universities and Colleges* (1968). A leader in the scientific community, Alvin Weinberg, has expressed his *Reflections on Big Science* (MIT Press, 1968), and agencies such as Brookings Institution have published important symposia, exemplified by Harold Orlans' *Science Policy and the University* (1968). A major feature of much of this literature published since 1965 is the expressed gradual awareness that the days of foundation and federal largesse are over, and that perhaps some science and research ought properly to be withdrawn from university supervision.

Each year for the past five years has seen a steady flow of books, articles, conference papers and the like describing types of institutions. There are the published and locally produced institutional self-studies; the conference discussions, such as those held by the American Association of Junior Colleges and the state associa-

Trends in the Literature 1965-1970

tions of junior colleges; and the monographs which attempt to characterize various types of institutions. Several books deal specifically with predominantly Negro colleges and a rather intensive debate conducted in print was stimulated by an essay on the predominantly Negro colleges published in the *Harvard Educational Review*. Junior colleges have received the largest volume of book-length treatments; Clyde Blocker et al., *The Two-Year College: A Social Synthesis* (Prentice-Hall, 1965), is illustrative. Church-related colleges have been the focus of several studies as have private liberal arts colleges, and these results have been widely disseminated through conference proceedings, journal articles and books. Morris Keeton and Conrad Hilberry in *Struggle and Promise: A Future for Colleges* (McGraw-Hill, 1969) exemplify high quality publication. Some of the religious denominations concerned with higher education have produced a reasonably steady body of literature, notably the Methodist Board of Higher Education and the higher education wing of the National Catholic Education Association. Academic deans of Jesuit institutions and writers for the *Benedictine Review* are examples of other elaborations and coverage. Although completed just at the beginning of the period treated in this essay, some mention should be made of the Library of Education Series produced by the Center for Applied Research in Education, Inc. This contains in relatively small books analyses of most of the existing types of institutions, ranging from the smaller liberal arts college to the technical institutes. One class of institution, rather than type, which has received a great deal of attention in virtually all literary media is the cluster or experimental college. As the full impact of large institutional size began to dawn on leaders in higher education, finding smaller units within which students could study or live seemed an imperative. This genre really began in the late 1950s when a series of institutional studies sponsored by the Ford Foundation resulted in the creation of New College at Hofstra University, Monteith College at Wayne State University, and eventually the creation of Hampshire College in Amherst, Massachusetts. However, other institutions then joined in the quest for new groupings, with widely publicized results, so that by 1970 Santa Cruz and Justin Morrill because almost shorthand ways of describing the cluster college concept. The literature is primarily descriptive, but some philosophic justification has been attempted, as in Warren Bryan Martin's two books, *Alternative to Irrelevance* (Abingdon, 1968) and *Conformity* (Jossey-Bass, 1969).

The last major category in this resumé subsumes physical plant, campus facilities, and the newer media for instruction. The safest generalization is that this literature is burgeoning, particularly that dealing with computers and other newer devices for instruction; and the literature seems represented equally in the various media. There are handbooks for the use of media, manuals designed to acquaint administrators with computer potentialities, conference summaries on uses of media, and attractively produced commercial brochures, guides, and handbooks designed to interest the educator in investment in hardware. The previously mentioned Educational Facilities Laboratories has sponsored major efforts at dissemination of information about facilities, much of which is based on great expertise and even some experimentation.

This essay is admittedly impressionistic and is designed to sketch only the broadest parameters of trends in the literature of higher education. It might, however, suggest elements which should be treated bibliographically in greater detail. The sheer volume and complexity of the literature dealing with student protest suggest that it deserves early systematic elaboration. Then the critical importance of statewide governance would seem to call for thorough bibliographic reference. Because of emerging significance, the curricula of professional schools ought to receive treatment ahead of the curricula of undergraduate education, especially since one major bibliographic essay on the undergraduate college is already available. Although the evaluative literature is still slight, general interest in interdisciplinary work, especially black studies, would make that topic an appropriate one for early elaboration. Because so little experimentation is actually going on regarding college teaching and because several essays have already summarized what is known, the subject of college teaching at this time does not seem to warrant extensive analysis, nor does the subject of the preparation

Trends in the Literature 1965–1970

of college teachers. Perhaps by 1975 this picture will have changed. Also to be postponed for several years should be literature regarding campus governance. Of course, this subject is of intense immediate interest and much experimentation is taking place. However, several years' experience with new forms would seem desirable before a major bibliographic essay is attempted.

Two

LITERATURE OF 1971

For neither the national economy nor the literature of higher education was 1970 a banner year. There were a few bright spots. Both the Carnegie Commission on Higher Education, through its official publisher McGraw-Hill, and Jossey-Bass produced needed and good quality statements and reports. There were a few serious attempts made by well-known spokesmen to leave lasting statements of interpretation and belief—Samuel Gould, for example. But overall there was a tired quality to the work. So much had been said since 1964 about the vexing problems that few could add any-

Literature of 1971

thing new. There was little which looked forward to the decade of the seventies with joy or anticipation, nor was there much praise for the genuine accomplishments of the sixties.

The mode of selecting books for comment is neither random nor comprehensive; hence no hard inferences can be drawn from numbers of books produced in various categories. But some speculation is possible. Governance perplexes, and while no definitive statements have yet appeared, the sixteen books imply a real questing for answers. Perhaps indicative of the general pensive mood are the twelve historical works, among which institutional histories predominate. Next in order is the hopefully declining topic of campus unrest, with work of outstanding merit and of abject silliness represented. A number of presidents added to the reflective literature by publishing their speeches given during the past decade or so—perhaps, the thought intrudes, as swan songs. Following are the categories dealing with types of institutions, the ever-present conference proceedings, teaching and other professional practice, and curricular matters; last but far from least are the six books using economic modes of analyses to examine the assumptions and practices of higher education.

Perspective may be provided by pondering subjects not well represented in the 1970 output which in the past have received intensive treatment. High on that list are international affairs and science policy. Futuristic and utopian literature did not appear as it has in the recent past. While eight books are classified under the heading of curriculum, considerable wrenching was necessary to group them so. The undergraduate curriculum, considering the amount of attention given to it in the reforming polemic, seemed strangely underrepresented. Similarly, the student personnel movement was not stressed nor were the newer media of instruction.

Added perspective can be gained by considering gaps in the literature which have not been filled this year or in years past. If there is a theory of organization or management which could be applied to higher education it is certainly not discussed in the literature. If psychology has a contribution to the practice of education, its spokesmen are strangely quiet. If philosophy has something to

The Literature of Higher Education 1971

say regarding the nature of higher education and its purposes, it must be speaking to a different audience. And if special education for minority group students is an expanding field, writers have not kept pace with the movement. It is true in this regard that there have been a number of books dealing with black experience, black history or black problems. But these have been issued without specific reference to institutionalized higher education.

One more point before turning to the literature itself. Little of what is produced is of high intellectual order. Certainly, the insightful statements of a Newman, Whitehead or Veblen find no competition. Nor have many distinguished members of other intellectual branches addressed themselves to higher education. Writers, historians, governmental theorists or spokesmen, and people active in the arts simply have not focused attention on higher education, although clearly colleges and universities should be important to them.

Three

GOVERNANCE

This category is not only the largest but also contains the best of the literature in 1970. Willingham's careful analysis of access, Dressel's insight about departments, and Eulau's view of legislative attitude are all excellent and add greatly to available knowledge.

> James M. Buchanan, Nicos E. Devletogolu
> **ACADEMIA IN ANARCHY**
> New York: Basic Books, 1970

These two extremely capable iconoclasts accept the premise that institutions of higher education are in chaos and then suggest that this can be explained in terms of elementary economics. Education is not a free good. That is, it does not abound in nature in unlimited quantities. Hence it can be considered as any other marketable commodity desired by people. Yet education is given deliberately and artificially three characteristics which distinguish it from other commodities: those who consume its product do not purchase it; those who produce it do not sell it; and those who finance it do not control it. The implications of these three differences are enormous. Since education cannot be obtained by all who desire it and since the consumer does not actually purchase the commodity, difficulties within the system develop. Available facilities become congested and the commodity is rationed frequently by irrational or inconsistent means. Thus free tuition, which is the device used to encourage this dysfunction, is deceiving. In a very general way, subsidization of university students by the general taxpayer amounts to transfer of wealth from the poor to the rich, and because students do not pay for their education they tend to treat the university, its faculty and facilities as if little or no scarcity value attaches to them. Thus students could be expected to judge their educational facilities as of less worth than their own automobile.

Many complaints about so-called irrelevant curriculum are based on the students' perception that curricula are tailored to considerations other than their own desires which they can express only with difficulty. Since faculty members are on tenure, in payment for which they accept slightly less money than they could obtain in other markets, and since the product they produce is designed to fit their own desires, faculty members are not directly harmed when student demonstrations and strikes break out. Not being definitely affected, they are not inclined to get too excited about the situation and hence not particularly willing to support administration in bringing protests under control. In the light of a number of economic principles, the authors generalize that under present conditions internal constitutional change in the university will be both limited in scope and tardy in coming. Faculty members will oppose changes which introduce indirect consumer controls. One agency, however, which could bring about university reform is the board of trustees. If the trustees reassert their control over the university they may yet be able to provide conditions by which a consistent set of economic principles can operate. The insights of this book are significant and conform to insights of other critics. By implication the authors move toward increases in tuition. They explicitly find some faculties resistant to change, and they correctly sense the theoretical significance of boards of trustees. They should be listened to; whether they will be is of course another matter.

M. M. Chambers
HIGHER EDUCATION IN THE FIFTY STATES
Danville, Ill.: Interstate, 1970

The author continues his prodigious labor for higher education with this veritable tour de force of factually sound, well written vignettes of public higher education in each of the fifty states. In each, the author deals with systems of governance, levels of support, shifting directions of effort, and implicitly some assessment of how successful or unsuccessful efforts have been. However, one theme or point of view seems to run throughout the book—a considerable skepticism of the values of tightly controlled systems of higher education. This is no new position for Chambers to hold; hence it is to be expected and in no way detracts from the solid scholarship on which the book is based. Such a document could be put to many uses, but certainly every actual and aspiring student of higher education should have mastered this work simply to have an appropriate context for thinking about the many issues involved. It could be used for a survey course or for an analytical seminar on higher education.

Commission on the Government of the
University of Toronto
TOWARD COMMUNITY IN UNIVERSITY GOVERNMENT
Toronto: University of Toronto Press, 1970

This book illustrates once more that a number of the Canadian institutions are making more thoughtful progress toward educational reform than are we. The authors describe various parts of the University of Toronto and then recommend changes in governance. They believe that older styles of control through lay boards are inappropriate and that some sort of fused controlling body, including lay, faculty, and political points of view, should be created. Democracy is to be insured by participation of both faculty and students at all levels of organization. However, these recommendations do not push to the absurd limit of participatory democracy. Thus, the commissioners see that students appropriately should have voice over some areas and that faculty should have voice over others. And the other elements of the reform movement in higher education are also reflected. Long-range planning is seen to be a good which must be arranged. Superinstitutional agencies for coordination and control seem inevitable, and any system of governance must accommodate them. Generally, secrecy in governance should be avoided and virtually all council or other organizational meetings should be open to the public. Rotation of department heads is preferable to long tenure, and even presidents should be appointed for specified terms. Because of the format of discussion-description argument, then recommendation, the book reads a little slowly; but if one can overcome that problem, the substance is well worth the time spent.

William L. Deegan, T. R. McConnell,
Kenneth P. Mortimer, Harriet Stull
JOINT PARTICIPATION AND
DECISION MAKING
Berkeley: Center for Research and Development
in Higher Education, 1970

From California comes a group of papers analyzing faculty government and faculty administration at Fresno State College. It is interesting commentary about one institution although it reveals possibly more about the attitudes of those who wrote the material than about Fresno State. Apparently, Fresno State began a study of governance at about the time the Center for Research and Development in Higher Education began to look at governance broadly. Representatives of the center visited Fresno State, interviewed people, examined documents and came out with a text which favored an academic assembly and senate, the use of students in governance, elected committees having heavy faculty representation, and in general supported a shared responsibility sort of governance. But the committee seemed to downgrade the actual and even potential role of college and university presidents. They say that most acts of leadership are not dramatic and that the era of the administrative giant has ended. This is, of course, conventional wisdom first promulgated by Clark Kerr, who visualized a university president as something not unlike a chairman of a board of directors. However, other models are still available and might have been given more thorough analysis. Parenthetically, a highly competent president of Fresno State left partly because his necessary powers had been so eroded by shared responsibility that he could no longer function effectively. The book is in soft cover and photo-offset print, presumably revealing an intention to restrict circulation. However, it could be of great value, particularly in courses dealing with college administration, for presenting one consistent point of view regarding governance. It should not be used alone, for there are other sides to the story.

Paul L. Dressel, F. Craig Johnson, Philip M. Marcus
THE CONFIDENCE CRISIS
San Francisco: Jossey-Bass, 1970

A data- and observation-based analysis of academic departments is presented here. Using teams of experienced observers, the authors sought to gain a notion of the role departments played in fifteen universities and their effect on the educational program, the stature of the institution, and relationships between people. Generally they find the not unexpected, that the academic department has emerged or is emerging as perhaps the controlling structure for institutional destinies. The work generally seems to confirm the hypotheses upon which the study was based. First, departments with high national standing, based on productivity and research and doctoral degrees, are characterized by more informal administrative organization and practices than departments of less stature. Second, departments of high national standing are less involved in local institutional matters and tend to ignore or evidence disdain for institutional practices.

> *Generally, the thing which distinguishes how department heads operate and the role departments play in determining the destiny of an institution is not any of the traditional distinctions, e.g., public versus private support, or church related versus secular, but rather the ranking of the institution on the Cartter Study of graduate excellence. In a very real sense the most influential institutions are now operating out of control because of the power of departments, and institutions are searching for ways to reestablish order without yielding the very real strengths which departmentalism provides. One device which apparently has been attempted in some institutions to break the hegemony of departments has been to create or to tolerate the evolution of separate institutes in the hopes that these could become centers for interdisciplinary education. Unfortunately the prevailing pattern is for these institutes to become institutionalized and to begin functioning as just one other department, most responsive to off-campus sources of funds and less responsive to the needs of on-campus students.*

While the tone of the book is generally critical, it is not vindictively so. Indeed, the experience of the study may have softened the senior author's well-known attitudes toward departments. He sees, for example, that frequently departments are enticed into their destructive independence by actions of central administration itself seeking "institutional excellence." The book is one of the relatively few produced each year which could be called a genuine contribution to substantive knowledge about the functioning of American education.

Stanley Elam, Michael H. Moskow, eds.
EMPLOYMENT RELATIONS IN HIGHER EDUCATION
Bloomington, Ind.: Phi Delta Kappa, 1969

Beyond doubt, this is one of the best available collections of papers dealing with current problems of governance in higher education. Several positions are enunciated in a brilliant essay by Harry Marmion showing how the AAUP has gradually moved from preoccupation with violations of academic freedom to a union-like stance regarding collective negotiation. Yet the AAUP has moved in this direction grudgingly. Myron Leiberman, in his usually perceptive fashion, has argued that shared responsibility in academic governance is really a tautology and that some form of representational system engaged in adversary relationships with management or central administration is the only consistent way to handle university organizations. People from the NEA in the conference seemed to be saying collective negotiations, collective bargaining, even the strike, were appropriate techniques but that the NEA or some of the state education associations were doing it better than the AFT. Several speakers, however, disagreeing with the adversary style, urged shared responsibility, which really means cutting down on the amount of power which central administration can use and assigning much of that to new faculty organizations. The issues are all clearly revealed in this collection of papers but by no means resolved. The one missing element was a forceful presentation favoring strong central government. Nonetheless, this book is the best to come along.

Heinz Eulau, Harold Quinley
STATE OFFICIALS AND HIGHER EDUCATION
New York: McGraw-Hill, 1970

The Literature of Higher Education 1971

This is a report of an intensive interview and questionnaire study of the attitudes, opinions, and information about higher education among legislators in selected states. The authors contend that their book makes no contribution to theoretical scholarship but does provide some information which might be useful. Here, I think the authors protest overmuch. It is just possible that in the long sweep of history this document may far outshadow the authors' more respectable theoretical fulminations. The pattern which emerges shows legislators, particularly those in responsible positions, aware of higher education, proud of their state's achievements, and willing within reason to try to find the resources needed by higher education. They are also willing to allow institutions and systems of institutions reasonable control over ongoing educational activity, with legislators providing funds and setting broad statewide policy. However, legislators not in critical positions seemingly know little about higher education, nor do legislators generally feel their constituencies are much aware of or concerned about colleges and universities. Higher education does not really have or serve as an important political constituency. Hence, on any critical controversy, legislators would be much more inclined to respond to the pressures of the politically potent than to the educational segment of society. Legislators were concerned about student dissent and felt that if local campus administrators did not control it some other agency would. Yet the quoted comments reveal much less vindictiveness on the part of legislators than some academicians claim is present. Legislators are much more understanding of student unrest than is the general public. This could become one of the more useful books to be sponsored by the Carnegie Commission on Higher Education.

JB Lon Hefferlin, Ellis L. Phillips, Jr.
INFORMATION SERVICES FOR ACADEMIC ADMINISTRATION
San Francisco: Jossey-Bass, in press

The authors report on the information currently available to colleges and universities and on the kinds that would be most helpful. The amount of information which crosses a president's desk on any given day is enormous, but much of it is unusable. The bulk of most frequently used information is informal and quite unsystematic. There is a tremendous need for systematic knowledge as institutions and their problems become increasingly complex. Quite clearly, simple expansion of the amount of information available is not needed. There is already more than can be digested. Rather, there is a need for metainformation, information about information. Existing sources seem inadequate for this purpose. Perhaps this need for information about information can be met best by the creation of a metainformation center, which will know where data, expertise, and additional knowledge can be obtained, and which can provide this information through personal contact with those who have it. Already a few people in the country seem to have at their personal disposal a great deal of knowledge about what information exists. What the authors propose is using to the full these relatively few people whose experiences have given them important information.

Asa S. Knowles
HANDBOOK OF COLLEGE AND
UNIVERSITY ADMINISTRATION
New York: McGraw-Hill, 1970

In two volumes Knowles brings together most of what is known about the subject. It is comprehensive, well written, and well edited. One dean who had not experienced the higher education literature remarked that for his purposes the handbook supplied at least a third of what he needed to know about any administrative query he chose to put to the test.

Dwight R. Ladd
CHANGE IN EDUCATIONAL POLICY
New York: McGraw-Hill, 1970

Through a number of case studies Ladd has established several things which many have long suspected. Institutional self-studies are laborious undertakings involving many different techniques, none of which have been completely validated. They usually produce countless recommendations which are extremely difficult to implement. Self-studies were originally encouraged primarily because of institutional needs to gain regional or special accreditation. However, since the outbreak of student protest in the mid-1960s, a number of institutions have been making serious attempts to study themselves as a basis for restructuring. Ladd selected several institutions of different types which had recently completed self-studies. He read through the reports and then spent some time on each campus talking with people who had participated in the study and forming judgments as to what had happened and what was likely to happen in the future. He found that institutions went about self-study differently, but generally some form of ad hoc committee or council was appointed and given the responsibility for conducting the study and for securing necessary data from other units in the institution. The overarching contribution of this book to theory of academic life is to call into serious question whether collegiality, in the sense of shared responsibility, can operate in such a complex undertaking as studying a full institution and charting its course. The results of most of these surveys were quite lackluster and contained many proposals not acted upon. Since many of the recommendations seemed to be reasonably well founded, the author raises the question as to whether presently available techniques for achieving consensus can operate. If, as he surmises, we have reached a limit of collegiality, then other patterns for educational policy must be developed. The author favors something akin to the responsible government of the parliamentary democracies. This system recognizes that after appropriate consultation someone must have the power to make decisions. Thus he would want to see, on such a matter as recommendations from a self-study, administrative officers of various sorts consulting with faculty groups and then actually putting something into effect. Of the many recent books dealing with governance, this one seems to have uncovered the most critical issues and in the long run will be of great value.

Governance

Earl J. McGrath
SHOULD STUDENTS SHARE THE POWER?
Philadelphia: Temple University Press, 1970

With this small book, McGrath has added one more document to his enormous contribution. In his usual careful fashion, he reviews the history of student participation in academic governance and points out how medieval university students in the south of Europe did maintain power and that periodically in subsequent centuries students have had considerable say, not only in their extra-class lives but with respect to the curriculum as well. Further, the several clear examples in the history of American higher education where students did have a major role in governance are proof to McGrath that students can act responsibly and well. The author tries to be objective in analyzing and criticizing the various arguments, pro and con, for the use of students in governance. However, his own preference for including students seems to shine through. Thus he quickly disposes of the contrary arguments that students will dominate the academic society, that students are immature, that they have such a brief tenure on campus, that they might act in ignorance of professional values, and that participation in governance might interfere with study or gainful employment. However, he doesn't deal with the possibility that a university could be considered a professional, service-providing agency not unlike a hospital, court or clinic, and that professional decisions theoretically should be made by professionals. Nor does he enter into any broad-scale assessment of how students in fact have performed outside of the relatively few institutions in which participation has long been a cardinal item of faith. Once McGrath establishes that students could and very likely should participate in governance, he then takes the next and quite valuable step of describing the techniques by which more participation could be brought about. "The experience of a few American institutions and some Canadian universities suggests that a governmental structure which assembles all the constituent parties in some organization like a Senate, including the Board, the administrators and the students in policy discussion, is better than one which provides for the reconciliation of opposing views after the constituent groups have taken independent action."

Sigmund Nosow
PROFESSIONAL SELF IMAGES AND ORGANIZATION ORIENTATIONS OF A GENERAL EDUCATION FACULTY
East Lansing: University College, Michigan State University, 1969

This is a sociological interpretation of the questionnaire study conducted among the faculty of Michigan State University's University College. The University College is perhaps the oldest and most successful institutionalized attempt to provide general education for students. This separate college, created in the 1940s with its own dean, faculty and budget, offered a prescribed program required of all degree candidates at Michigan State. In an effort to plan for the future and to identify tensions and problems, this study was undertaken. It establishes that there is still more satisfaction among faculty in a college which does not offer a degree program, but they are searching for greater variety and for ways to satisfy other professional desires. People in the humanities departments seem more satisfied with the present structure, and older faculty members—those who have been there almost since the organization of the college—seem more satisfied than the more recently trained ones. The University College has clearly been affected by the tendencies toward greater specialization and professionalization in the late 1950s and '60s, brought about in part because faculty members have received different training and partly because Michigan State University has embarked on a comprehensive graduate professional and research effort. Given the questing of faculty members for greater variety in professional activity, the first palliative seems to be to expand the presently prescribed four courses into a number of different course options, so that individual faculty members can teach things closer to their own professional training and students can feel there is some choice open to them.

Having made several rudimentary studies similar to this one, I had the distinct impression that I had seen much of the evidence before. Nosow's statement, "While student reactions to the basic college are relatively favorable, and very favorable for the humanities curricula, the lack of clarity about educational objectives which students generally have are also evinced in their responses to the specific general education courses," seems to paraphrase almost exactly sentences I wrote in 1948. Nonetheless, the effort must be praised. It would seem that this constant search for evidence may in part be responsible for a generally innovative spirit which characterizes Michigan State University.

Stephen H. Spurr
ACADEMIC DEGREE STRUCTURES:
INNOVATIVE APPROACHES
New York: McGraw-Hill, 1970

This book, one more in the series of reports sponsored by the Carnegie Commission on Higher Education, presents a one-man analysis of the history of academic degrees, the present range of academic degrees offered, and some recommendations for a future system of degrees which would bring some order out of seeming chaos. The issues, some implicitly and others explicitly discussed, are the obvious ones. Are there too many different degrees? What should be the role or meaning of a master's degree in the arts and sciences? Is there room now for an intermediate degree between the master's and the doctorate? What sorts of honorary degrees should be produced or granted? And is the time ripe for some degree beyond the PhD which would signify even greater attention given to research competency? In analyzing these issues, the author attends to some unsuccessful reforming efforts. Thus he finds that the attempt to collapse the baccalaureate degree at the University of

Chicago was unsuccessful, and that efforts to make respectable the master's degree in arts and sciences have not worked out. The book's thesis is that there should be a reasonably systematic outline of degree structures with specific characteristics: the number of different degree titles should be kept as low as possible; degree structure should be flexible in time; and each degree should represent a definite termination point with no implied assumption that a further degree was really required. From these principles he develops a scheme which would show all students in collegiate programs moving toward the associate of arts degree, whether or not this was taken in a junior college. Next would come a bachelor's degree, followed by a master's degree, and then in some of the professional fields a specialist degree. After that he proposes an intermediate degree, particularly in the arts and sciences, which could be labeled a doctor, followed finally by the PhD or the appropriate doctorate in a professional field. Ideally, Spurr would like to see just a bachelor's degree, but recognizing the realities of academic life, he finds room for a bachelor of arts and a bachelor of science. About many of his recommendations there can be honest disagreement. For example, some will feel that emphasizing the associate of arts degree intensifies an unfortunate split between lower division and upper division work. Others are considerably more critical of the PhD, and quite a few are not sanguine that any kind of intermediate degree will actually take. But the book is informative. It is clearly, if not scintillatingly written, and well deserves a place in professional libraries.

Robert C. Ward
MR. PRESIDENT, THE DECISION IS YOURS. DEAL OUT THE DOUGH
Lexington: University of Kentucky, 1970

This is a paperbacked, offset-printed attempt to prove the values of program planning and budgeting, but like its many predecessors, it fails. Using clichés and jargon which is almost impossible to decipher, the author describes the flow of events from planning (which apparently is a long view) to programing the actual budgeting (a shorter view), which must take into consideration personal values. As in many other books dealing with this subject, the real meaning lies in the observation that if people have more and better information about a broader range of alternatives, they are likely to make better planning decisions than in the absence of information and alternatives. This, of course, is an important message. So much past budgeting seems to have assumed that once something is in existence it should continue in existence. A system of program and budgetary review which makes an administrator ponder whether a laboratory school or a center for urban studies should be supported seems sound. It would help, however, if the book made clear how the consideration of programs differs from the existing practice of asking oneself whether or not psychology, economics, mathematics, education and sociology should each offer work in statistics.

Myron F. Wicke
HANDBOOK FOR TRUSTEES
Nashville, Tenn.: Board of Education, The United Methodist Church, 1969

Wicke presents the conventional wisdom about lay boards of trustees—how they derive their authority from charters granted in one way or another by the state, and how they have the three principal missions of selecting a president, declaring institutional objectives and policies, and preserving and investing properties and funds of the institution. The revision of this generally useful little book was mandated by changes which have characterized higher education in the late 1960s. Yet careful reading of the handbook does not reveal that Wicke has developed ideas for student participation in governance or faculty involvement at the highest level. A serious criticism is that the old system of legitimacy which the board of trustees personified was no longer appropriate and that a new system of legitimacy should be contrived. Significantly, the author did not comment at some length on recent findings which suggest that boards of trustees in aggregate represent a most limited segment of the population. While Morton A. Rauh's book is included in a brief reading list, the substance of that work is not indicated in the handbook; yet given the times, those findings are of considerable importance. Still, of the twelve studies in Christian Higher Education published by the Methodist Board of Higher Education, this seems by far the most complete and the most useful. A copy should be given to each new board member at the time he assumes his duties.

Warren W. Willingham
FREE ACCESS TO HIGHER EDUCATION
New York: College Entrance Examination Board, 1970

The author's intent is to show just how accessible higher education is. After reviewing the public drift toward acceptance of the principle of equal opportunity of higher education, Willingham both defines what he means by accessibility and makes rather explicit his own value stance that open access is desirable. Essentially, a free access college is one which has relatively low tuition and relatively low selectivity and which is located close to where students are. The mode of study consisted of relating, state by state, the existence of free access institutions to population figures. The results of this effort are presented in a state-by-state analysis with an indication of additional institutions that would be needed if goals of increasing the number of free access institutions were to be achieved. In aggregate Willingham finds that slightly more than two out of five people live within commuting distance of a free access college in the United States. However, a serious deficiency of accessible higher education exists in twenty-three of the twenty-nine largest metropolitan areas in the country. The northeastern part of the United States demonstrates the most serious deficiency, while the West Coast has the most accessible colleges and the highest rate of college attendance generally, but with considerably lessened access within urban areas. The South seems covered by free access colleges, although de facto segre-

Governance

gation makes accessibility illusionary. The work is carefully done, and proper restraint is exercised in extrapolating policy recommendations. A major contribution of the study to the emerging theory of education is an attempt to analyze the concept of relevance, which results in a discussion of four broad types of relevance. This important study must undoubtedly have been an expensive one, so the College Entrance Examination Board should be especially commended for bringing it to the attention of the profession.

Four

✯✯✯✯✯✯✯✯✯✯✯✯✯✯✯

HISTORY

✯✯✯✯✯✯✯✯✯✯✯✯✯✯✯

Generally, these works are competent but relatively minor additions. They add to the literature but in the long run will best achieve their purpose when they are used to enrich broader historical interpretations. Thus, there is a real place for institutional histories, but for most readers these become significant in larger contexts.

> Frank K. Burrin
> EDWARD CHARLES ELLIOTT, EDUCATOR
> Lafayette, Ind.: Purdue University Studies, 1970

This doctoral dissertation is an official biography of an important president of Purdue University. The significance of the study is that it typifies much of the history of education during the first half of the twentieth century in the United States. Edward Charles Elliott was born in 1874 in the Midwest, proceeded through grammar school and high school and attended the University of Nebraska. After graduation he entered public school teaching in Colorado, became superintendent of the Leadville schools and began to think deeply about the problems of education. He early became acquainted with the reforming leaders, such as Dewey and Cubberley, and began not only to put some of their ideas into effect but to theorize and analyze things himself. From Colorado he moved to the University of Wisconsin in the department of education, thence to the presidency of the University of Montana, and finally to Purdue University. Throughout this significant career, he wrote about such matters as school surveys, the attempts to provide a scientific basis for education, theories of educational administration, accreditation, grading practices—indeed, almost every issue then being raised in education. In time, he shifted his analytical talent and focused on problems of colleges and universities. He was one of the earliest to analyze systematically boards of trustees. He produced important works on the government of higher education and was one of the founding authors of a periodical compendium on "The Colleges and the Courts." After retirement from the presidency of Purdue, he, like many others of the same type, continued an active professional life as consultant and official in various professional organizations. The author deliberately (apparently at Elliott's request) devotes little space to the subject as a human being. Hence there is an arid quality to the writing. Elliott doesn't really come through as a flesh-and-blood man. However, this weakness is rectified by the detailed description of a career slope and an indication of the contributions of one man to an emerging educational ethos.

Louis G. Geiger
VOLUNTARY ACCREDITATION
Chicago: The North Central Association of Colleges and Secondary Schools, 1970

The Literature of Higher Education 1971

The writing about accreditation in education is generally about as dreary as one can find, but Geiger has managed to create a thoroughly readable and informative book. The North Central Association is the largest and beyond doubt the most influential of the six regional accrediting agencies. Before World War II, it had already established an enviable record of developing policies which led to the gradual upgrading of many colleges in the twenty-one states which comprise it. After World War II, facing the many profound changes which were taking place in education and in the nation, the Association began to adjust and to create new modes and roles for itself. By developing a commission on research and service, it created an agency which could do much more than simply maintain standards. That commission could render a variety of direct services to both secondary schools and colleges. To illustrate, the North Central Study on Liberal Arts was a self-perpetuating device to help weaker collegiate institutions in the region improve themselves and thereby to produce better teachers for the public schools. Sensing its increased significance, the association took the lead in developing a federation of accrediting agencies which would allow the autonomy of the six regional associations to be maintained, yet would have a voice at the highest national level.

If the book has a significant weakness, it lies with the overly commendatory stance toward the North Central Association. It is true that the association has done much good, yet as a human agency it is far from perfect. A little more candor might have made the work still more significant. For example, the author doesn't really indicate why the executive board overruled the recommendation of a visiting committee to continue the probationary status of Parsons College. Going into some of the sheer human irritation which that act revealed might have been healthy. Then, too, the subject provided an opportunity for the author to examine in greater detail the strengths and weaknesses of the accreditation process. One comes away from reading this book feeling that while some changes have been made, there is general satisfaction with the techniques of visitation, self-study, and review as they are presently practiced. But these are relatively minor caveats. The author set out to document

History

the evolution of one instrumentality of the educational establishment, and he has done so admirably. The other accrediting associations might consider commissioning similar works, for in aggregate they could contribute much to understanding the past twenty-five years.

Oscar and Mary F. Handlin
THE AMERICAN COLLEGE AND AMERICAN CULTURE
New York: McGraw-Hill, 1970

The authors' intent is to clarify the role of socialization in the development of the college in the United States. Without rejecting other purposes, the essay attempts to show how college attendance has historically been a part of the socialization process, and that changes in colleges can be largely attributable to changes in the society to which individuals must relate and accommodate themselves. Thus early colonial colleges stressed religion, discipline and a missionary spirit which were characteristic of the entire English colonial new world struggling to create a different sort of society. Colonial colleges were ideally organized and conducted to serve as asylums for young boys from a growing middle class in America. Thus New England colleges were somewhat nonutilitarian in preparing students for a later vocation but were highly utilitarian in fulfilling a custodial role. The rapid increase in the number of institutions in the United States after 1770 is accounted for by the expansion of the nation, an emergent virulent nationalism and a growing awareness that colleges could really help a person earn a better living. Then, from 1870 to the mid-twentieth century the form and influence of American institutions were determined by the rapid industrialization of the country and the need to socialize people into an urban civilization. The earlier morality inculcated in students by colleges gave way and institutions for a time almost abdicated any concern for the out-of-class life of students because of a general lack of agreement on conventional moral wisdom. The authors select as the next great period the decades 1930 to 1960; they admit this was a period full of paradoxes but it did seem to present a new consensus with which institutions had to contend. By 1930 it seemed clear that individual entrepreneurship was not the route most people would take toward achievement. Rather would large organizations provide the opportunities. Hence the institutions came to take on a more bureaucratic cast to prepare people for this new style of life.

This book is a short essay which gives the appearance of trying to compress the history of American higher education into a predetermined theoretical mold. The factual material seems accurate and the sense of changing institutions plausible; but one has a feeling that the periods used as a tool of analysis were selected for other purposes and the collegiate enterprise was simply forced into that structure. There are considerably better examples of intellectual history addressing problems of collegiate education.

Michael R. Harris
FIVE COUNTER REVOLUTIONISTS IN HIGHER EDUCATION
Corvallis: Oregon State University Press, 1970

Through detailed analysis of their voluminous writing, Harris links together Irving Babbitt, Albert J. Nock, Abraham Flexner, Robert Maynard Hutchins and Alexander Meiklejohn as having been generally opposed to the operationalism or the utilitarianism which has characterized American higher education. While Babbitt and Nock emerge as elitist, Meiklejohn and Hutchins, of course, sought a highly rational education which would be appropriate for all people. Babbitt wanted universities to discover cultural standards and the colleges to inculcate them in a limited number of the elect. Nock probably wanted a similar sort of system but was convinced that the destruction of the classical synthesis in the colonial college meant really the end of any viable American education.

History

Flexner, of course, strongly influenced by his early exposure to German universities, urged something like the ideals of the German university for the United States. Hutchins preoccupied himself with intellectual training and the great ideas which have shaped the Western world, while Meiklejohn felt that an intellectual examination of broad and complicated social issues could eventually bring about reform in the society. The author manages, for the most part, to keep his distance from these points of view but occasionally lapses and implies that while he recognizes the romanticism he still feels that these critics were on sound critical ground. The author concludes that none of these five individuals made lasting contributions of significance to the ongoing practice of higher education. Many of Hutchins' reforms at Chicago disappeared almost at the moment he left the institution. Meiklejohn's reforms were, for the most part, short-lived. American society is instrumentalist, pragmatic, and wants its institutions to contribute directly to ongoing events. Hence, these five were out of step with the society all along. The book is quite well written and makes a modest substantive contribution to intellectual history. Its contribution to the practices and processes of higher education is likely to be no more pronounced than were the ideas of his subjects.

James Koerner
THE PARSONS COLLEGE BUBBLE: A TALE OF HIGHER EDUCATION IN AMERICA
New York: Basic Books, 1970

Parsons College in Fairfield, Iowa, achieved national attention, fame, and ridicule under the leadership of Millard George Roberts, who became president of a weak but not really moribund school in 1955 and left it without accreditation, with heavy financial liabilities, and with a legacy of controversy, success, hatred, and press agentry in 1967. That a church-related college of small means and even smaller aspirations could become a national educational issue was in large part a product of a national mania for college degrees accompanied by a demand for higher education which seriously exceeded supply in the late 1950s. Publicity, regardless of whether good or bad, vigorous student recruitment, a year-round operation of the campus, streamlined curricula taught by three different types of faculty, rapid but cheap construction of physical plant, application of presumed new management techniques, and an open-door policy which would give students a second, third, or even fifteenth chance to achieve a degree and, of course, to provide the tuition needed for a self-supporting private college—these were the stuff of which the Parsons saga is composed. But President Roberts and through him Parsons College attracted enormous hatred and suspicion as well as considerable trust and respect. Throughout the most dramatic period of President Roberts' administration he and the college were involved in controversy with the North Central Association of Colleges and Secondary Schools, which, after a series of highly inconsistent acts, finally expelled the institution.

All of this history Koerner chronicles with considerable clarity and great insight. He shows that most of what Roberts tried has been and is being attempted elsewhere. Finally, however, after examining the matter as dispassionately as possible, Koerner believes it was right that Parsons College lost its accreditation and that President Roberts lost his job. But the way in which these events were brought about was questionable. The weakness of the book is that it still leaves central mysteries unsolved. Why did an accreditation team recommend public probation in the same year that accreditation was actually granted weaker institutions? What motivated some experienced observers to believe a crusade against Parsons was warranted while others of equal reputation could, even at the end, feel the experiment was exciting and would in the long run be worthwhile? Why did educational associations and their leaders become so upset about this man and his college yet not use a key instrument of the academy, the open forum, to explore Millard Roberts' ideas and practices? Only near the end was the American Association for Higher Education persuaded to allow Roberts a platform.

In a sense there are two major themes in the Parsons story.

History

There is the personality of President Roberts, and the author almost finds the essence of the man. But the other theme is the reaction of American leadership in higher education to Parsons College and to Roberts, and this is never brought into focus. There are also two major educational issues, either one of which could have been treated as central—the nature of collegiate innovation and the nature of accreditation. Koerner was unable to accomplish a fusion of the two and the book has a somewhat disjointed aura about it. But this book comes as close as any to being a definitive treatment of a minor but intriguing episode in American higher education. The details are accurate, the prose clear, and the treatment balanced. When the history of the reforming decade of the sixties is written, this work will be frequently cited.

David A. Lockmiller
SCHOLARS ON PARADE
London: Macmillan, 1970

Lockmiller has produced a minor but engaging contribution to the history of higher education. In chapters dealing with early European universities, English institutions, colonial institutions and contemporary higher education, the author presents a chronology of development, provides anecdotal material to give life to the institutions being described, and shows the ways in which degrees, robes and ceremonials evolved. In a sense, the book is an anecdotal chronical rather than a history, for the author does little to indicate social forces and pressures; and the book, by its nature, is without a central thesis. But these are not intended as negative comments, for the book doesn't pretend to be a major treatise in intellectual history. This book, together with Stephen Spurr's *Academic Degree Structure,* probably represents all most of us will ever need to know about this subject, although, of course, the issue as to whether or not degrees could be abolished is likely to receive considerable debate in the future.

The Literature of Higher Education 1971

Rayford W. Logan
HOWARD UNIVERSITY: THE FIRST HUNDRED YEARS, 1867–1967
New York: New York University Press, 1969

This is a commissioned work in the sense that it was prepared as part of the centennial celebration for Howard University. Hence its objectivity can be questioned. The author is a historian on the faculty who has done painstaking research in uncovering much of the minutia of the evolution of this predominantly Negro institution. Howard University came into existence as one of the activities of the Freedman's Bureau after the Civil War, and its first president and namesake was the head of that organization. Originally the institution was to have been a college concerned with the preparation first of preachers, then the preparation of teachers and preachers, on the assumption that these two met the greatest need of the Negro community. However, even before the institution opened its doors, wise decisions were made to call it a university, thus paving the way for gradual development of a reasonable complement of professional schools. In the beginning, or probably in the first flush of the end of the Civil War and a spirit of emancipation, there appears to have been no intent to design it solely for Negroes. However, as the nineteenth century wore on, and as segregation became imbedded first in practice and then in legislation, the university became fixed as a Negro institution offering one of the few ways by which black youth could develop professional competencies needed by the Negro community. In the early days, faculty, administration and board members were more likely to be white than black. However, by the turn of the century, Negroes were clearly in the majority.

Logan has added distinctively to the emerging literature about contributions of Negroes to American civilization. And, as a demonstration of the Negro community's struggles to develop adequate educational outlets, the discussions of the formative years are significant. The book begins to falter in its treatment of recent history which perhaps emphasizes more than other discussions the relevancy of Howard's administration and educational program to the aspirations of black militants, Black Power, and the civil rights movement. Comparing this interpretation with Lawrence B. De-Graf's "Howard: The Evolution of Black Student Revolt," in Foster and Long, *Protest: Student Activism in America,* makes the reader curious as to where truth really does lie. Since the book is institutional history and written for a ceremonial occasion, it is overly full of names of individuals and specific detail. It probably could have been cut in half and focused more on interpretation. However, detail is still needed, and this book should contribute to the work of those who may ultimately write a synthesis of the history of Negro education in America.

Philip S. Moore
A CENTURY OF LAW AT NOTRE DAME
Notre Dame: University of Notre Dame Press, 1969

Moore has produced a short, readable and quite insightful history. Treating the subject by eras ascribed to a series of deans, he traces the unlikely evolution of a law school in a church-related institution. He describes the educational innovations brought about by deans and in the last chapter on The Future presents what is almost a blueprint of reform within professional education. Thus the elective system has been reinstated, the study of law is more closely correlated with sociology and other social and behavioral sciences. Students are encouraged to learn off campus and there is a strong influx of materials from international affairs. This book, of course, is no major institutional history yet it is potentially of greater value than longer ones simply because the author is concerned with educational issues and uses his history to illustrate these.

Howard Osman, ed.
CONTEMPORARY CRITICS OF EDUCATION
Danville, Ill.: Interstate, 1970

The Literature of Higher Education 1971

The author presents under a single cover a number of the better known and more easily available criticisms of education from the elementary years on through graduate school. Just listing a few of the authors tells all there is to say about the content of the book: Bestor, Bruner, Hutchins, Goodman, Koerner, Rickover, Rafferty. Most of these critics seem more attuned to the point of view of the Council for Basic Education than with the several developmental schools of education: Sanford and Taylor are conspicuously absent. The purpose of the collection is unclear. If it is, as the editor says, "to present some of the major criticisms being leveled at contemporary education," the purpose has not comprehensively been achieved, nor are the uses to which such a book might be put immediately apparent.

Manuel P. Servin, Iris Higbie Wilson
SOUTHERN CALIFORNIA AND ITS
UNIVERSITY: A HISTORY OF U.S.C., 1880–1964
Los Angeles: Ward Ritchie Press, 1969

This book is a reasonably typical institutional history which will contain much of interest to people closely associated with the university, and some material which can be basic to broader historical analyses. The University of Southern California was founded in 1880 and evolved somewhat in the way other private universities developed during the last part of the nineteenth and early twentieth century. It came into existence as one more educational dream of the Methodist-Episcopal Church, which correctly guessed that southern California would ultimately expand into one of the more populous areas in the state. A university properly located could contribute to and gain from that expected growth. This tendency to deal in futures led to some of the early grandiose plans for expansion. The university even attempted a half-statewide system of education, conducted under private auspices but reflecting some of the diversity of type of institution which characterizes California education in the 1960s and '70s. Once the wildly speculative stage was

History

passed and binding decisions were made to maintain the original key location, expansion of the institution proceeded in a reasonably steady way through addition to the liberal arts curriculum and a rapid proliferation of professional schools. Some of these were ultimately found to be too expensive, such as medicine, which was turned over to the state of California. The university's periodical fund-raising attempts seem to have been somewhat unsuccessful. As was true of many other institutions, several strong presidents of considerable imagination and long tenure were the real builders of the university. Outstanding among these was Rufus Bernhard Von Kleinsmid who presided over pre-1919 affluence, Depression frugality, and World War II service. His concentration on building undoubtedly left the university with the basis for an effective physical plant; but his slow attention to faculty salaries, particularly in the immediate post-war period, probably contributed to a long-lasting academic weakness. In the 1950s, bitten by the quest-for-excellence virus, the university under new leadership attempted to become one of the major research centers in the nation. Even a successful fund drive was unable to overcome the inertia of prior faculty recruitment policies. The book is descriptive and filled with names of people who contributed to the growth of the university but seems somewhat short on analysis. Thus one would like to have seen more speculation on the effect of the creation of so many professional schools. The question is: does the attempt to maintain full professional coverage so drain an institution's resources and dynamics that it is forever prevented from sustained and focused growth?

G. Kerry Smith, ed.
TWENTY-FIVE YEARS: 1945–1970
San Francisco: Jossey-Bass, 1970

The book is essentially a collection of papers or addresses delivered at the annual conference on higher education sponsored by the American Association for Higher Education over the past twenty-five years. The papers each year are published in conference

The Literature of Higher Education 1971

proceedings under the title "Current Issues in Higher Education," and the present volume distills from those papers a view of the issues over a quarter of a century. Generally, these papers reveal three major divisions. The first, lasting to the mid-50s, is a period of hopeful supplication during which leaders were proclaiming what higher education could do for the society if resources were made available. Then came a period of fruition when higher education actually did receive the respect and support it wished for itself. A period of disillusionment and disenchantment followed when public backlash developed against the excesses and malfunctionings of colleges and universities. Since there are so many essays reflecting such rich insights, no short review can capture the spirit of all of them. However, the theoretical framework can be exposed by quotes from the first and last chapters.

> *The twenty-five years from 1945 to 1970 were perilous ones for higher education. That quarter century ushered in the atomic age with Hiroshima and shortly thereafter we felt the impact of a new breed of college student—the G.I., an older, serious learner who, more often than not, was quite willing to dispense with an education if he could effectively be prepared for a good job. Then came McCarthyism and civil rights, Sputnik, and the National Defense Education Act, sit-ins at Berkeley, Vietnam and, finally, most astonishing of all, a new breed of college student who was quite willing to postpone job training until later if only he could find a college or university to give him an education.*

And from the last chapter:

> *How central in the life of the nation will higher education be in the future? James Perkins expressed the dream of the 1960s with his remark that the American university had become the modern church and cathedral. Certainly it has become central in the production of workers and in the conduct of some research. But examined in the light of political power, social criticism, formation of national values, setting of standards of*

History

taste, or even affecting seriously the lives of its graduates, this desired centrality seems still remote. Only as higher education repairs its damaged credibility is it likely to become the true cathedral of a secular and sensate society.

Paul Woodring
INVESTMENT IN INNOVATION
Boston: Little, Brown, 1970

This book is a history and an interpretation of the Fund for the Advancement of Education. The fund was an early effort of the Ford Foundation to deal specifically with critical problems of education and to foster needed reform. Eventually, for a variety of reasons, the Fund for the Advancement of Education was collapsed into the Ford Foundation itself and became the department concerned with education. When the officers and directors of the foundation asked Paul Woodring to prepare a history, they obtained a person well acquainted with the whole educational scene, one intimately involved in Ford Foundation activities, and the rare sort of educator who writes exceedingly well and lucidly. However, they also obtained an author who would have to struggle for objectivity because of his long friendship with principals in the fund and involvement in foundation-supported activities. This difficulty becomes apparent in the author's treatment of two of the most influential individuals in the operation of the fund, Alvin Eurich and Clarence Faust. These men certainly have been powerful influences for reform and certainly directed the energies of the fund toward critical questions. But one does wonder whether either of the two might not have made at least a few mistakes. Over the years the fund sponsored attempts to improve the preparation of teachers, experimentation with television as an important medium of instruction, considerable experimentation with acceleration and early admission, and had begun some equal opportunity programs. During its productive years, the fund, as an operating agency, sponsored or actually produced some seminal works on education, including

General Education in School and College, which was the study upon which the concept of advanced placement was based, Oliver Carmichael's *Graduate Education Today,* which provided the intellectual base for the attempt (abortive, to be sure) to refurbish the master's degree as an appropriate teaching degree, and *Teacher Education Reappraisal,* which spoke to some of the criticisms Arthur Bestor and others earlier had advanced. Woodring believes that overall the fund was instrumental in producing a number of innovations some of which, it is true, might have happened anyway; and he does feel that the fund was properly experimental. An earlier president of the Ford Foundation had argued that a foundation should stay ahead but not too far ahead of the society. Woodring believes that the fund was frequently farther ahead than the foundation might have wished it to be. The total work is considerably better than most appraisals of institutions, and the interpretations might well assist other foundations planning agendas for the future.

Five

CAMPUS UNREST

The majority of these are edited volumes, one of which is excellent. But as is usual within collections, quality is uneven. Eventually, of course, a synthesis of the period of the late 1960s will be created by a single individual, but for the present, these discrete bits of wisdom and insight will have to suffice.

Joseph A. Califano, Jr.
THE STUDENT REVOLUTION: A GLOBAL CONFRONTATION
New York: Norton, 1970

The Literature of Higher Education 1971

Here is one more interpretation of what has happened on university campuses during the 1960s. The result is a generally conservative analysis and critique with a generally libertarian set of presuppositions. The method of study was quite casual, that is, visiting campuses in the United States and in Europe, talking with students and professors and then reflecting on what he thought was true. The common elements he finds in student protest everywhere are not particularly surprising—small numbers of hard-core radical students, fuzzy objectives reflecting a crisis of belief, time for revolt provided by affluence, a search for alternatives to a complex, technologically-based life. He also finds that escalations of protest follow quite similar patterns—a small group of radical students finds an issue which can broaden base of support, instant communications with a larger geographic area, followed by a mistake on the part of authorities. While there is much in common between American and European universities, there are significant differences. Foreign universities are not troubled by the black-white issue. The drug problem does not seem to be particularly acute abroad. While the Vietnam issue is operative both in the United States and abroad, it is not exacerbated by the threat of the draft. The foreign adult population does not seem to assign a conspiracy basis to student protest as do a large number of American adults. The most insightful portion of the book probes the crisis of belief, and the author quite rightly places considerable blame on rational and critical professors who have labeled as myth much belief but have not substituted anything for those ideas they destroyed.

Julian Foster, Durward Law, eds.
PROTEST: STUDENT ACTIVISM IN AMERICA
New York: William Morrow, 1970

Out of the enormous volume of anthology literature about student activism, this is by far the best collection. The editors have selected well from available literature, have organized the selections aptly and provide a coherent view of what has happened to American higher education since 1964. Clark Kerr indicates the accelerating rate of student protest and predicts no appreciable let-up in the future. The editors summarize and present other essays emphasizing the now well-accepted description of protesting students as bright, intellectually oriented, well-adjusted young people from liberal and professional homes, and indicating that an institution's proneness to protest is somewhat related to the proportion of such students enrolled. But this book is no collection of dry, empirical data. Several thoughtful speculative articles, searching for underlying sources of whatever might be the ideology of the new student, and the well-developed case study interpretation provide meaning in depth for student protest. Nor do the editors neglect the need for practical recommendations. They have selected normative material indicating how administrators have responded to protest activities and derived from these some guidelines which administrators might consider in the future. Thus they suggest that in some situations when activists intend to demonstrate an administrative response might be to offer cooperation in the enterprise. This may sound Machiavellian, but those institutions which have developed guidelines in advance have seemingly experienced less serious outbreaks than those which have not planned ahead. If an administrator wishes help in these troublous times, this book should be required reading.

Arlene Kaplan Daniels, Rachel Kahn-Hut and Associates
ACADEMICS ON THE LINE
San Francisco: Jossey-Bass, 1970

This group of teachers have made a book and they probably should not have done so. It is a hodgepodge of reflections, theorizing and exhortations regarding the strike at San Francisco State College in 1968–69. The contributors attempt to explain why they left their traditional roles as teachers, joined the AFT and went out on strike. They see themselves as having gradually been impressed by the rightness of many student dissatisfactions, and having reached a gradual awareness that the California State College System was simply too rigid to respond to student needs. The fact that striking teachers used bread-and-butter issues of salaries and working conditions as their principal demands is explained away as a subterfuge to obtain strike approval from the San Francisco Labor Council; but there is only the simple assertion to prove that this is the case. Presumably, a chronology of events was intended to emerge from this collection of impressionistic papers but this intent was not realized. Thus, a chapter describing the experimental college as a needed innovation in an otherwise grim state institution flows into a panegyric on the camaraderie faculty members developed on the picket line. Immediately following is a polemic which tries to show that the contemporary university attempting to be true to its presumed scholarly traditions is denying large segments of the population the chance to obtain what they hoped the university could provide them. The old saw as to whether there could be a value-free social science is debated without resolution, and this somewhat unsatisfying section is followed by three chapters which belabor the obvious—that faculty members in the past have not had much real power, can be accused of acting irresponsibly, and must, regardless of personal desires, function within a bureaucracy. One supposes this is intended to be a revolutionary document but it is neither persuasive as to the effectiveness of the techniques, such as a strike, nor edifying in interpreting the strike itself.

Lawrence E. Eichel and Others
THE HARVARD STRIKE
Boston: Houghton Mifflin, 1970

The authors have produced a readable and valuable chronicle of one important episode in the history of student dissent. While generally sympathetic with the aims of striking students, they still manage to portray reality. They see Harvard as being a highly selective institution which nevertheless became more and more unresponsive to the fundamental needs of undergraduate students in the middle 1960s. Student irritation and frustration were brought into focus by American foreign policy, the university involvement in national affairs, and ROTC training and activated by the relatively few radicals organized in SDS. After a series of events involving the maintenance of ROTC, SDS was able to generate sufficient student support to conduct the occupation of University Hall. They were enabled to do this partly because there was no faculty mechanism which consistently could respond to demands about ROTC and by the confluence of several relatively minor but related events, such as the reduction of scholarships held by students who had been placed on probation and the importation and subsequent arrest of a radical student from Columbia. Finally, since the real administrative power of Harvard, which lay in the hands of the president and the Council of Deans, seemed out of touch with student feelings, frustrations led students to the occupation of a building. Subsequently, the president and council decided (in implementation of long-existing plans) to call for police help in clearing the building. The student strike, the catharsis of mass meetings and passing of resolutions, and the virtual disavowal of presidential leadership by a faculty vote completed the upheaval. The results seem generally to have been negative. The faculty came perilously close to becoming polarized; conditions of student living did not appear to have been changed; and while ROTC was discredited and removed, the war in Vietnam continues. The book is clearly a superior interpretation of an episode from the '60s and will very likely become essential secondary evidence for future more national interpretations.

Janet Harris, ed.
STUDENTS IN REVOLT
New York: McGraw-Hill, 1970

One can only hope that this is one of a decreasing number of pretentious presentations of polemics by protesting students. The context is seen as a worldwide student revolt which by challenging traditional values compels society and the state to accept inevitable

The Literature of Higher Education 1971

transformation. Young people all over the world are seen as demanding freedom to think, speak, and learn, and as discarding authoritarian values. Students refuse to accept the social and intellectual control of a society which gives them no part in making decisions. They oppose war, are anti-imperialist and reject institutions. Although the student activists are small in number, their impact is large. They presumably have brought the issues in modern society starkly into the open. They have discarded the old view of the university as an ivory tower and have presented a challenge for the future. One of the more thoughtful pieces in the collection is a short introductory essay which does manage to convey how world technology has changed in just over a decade. But this is followed by a romantic plea by the writer of the essay.

> *If hatred is what you want then stick with the old institutions for they are full of it. But comrade across the time barrier, I believe you want to make a new world and you have the power to do it. You do not need guns—you need courage to walk without guns. If you want a world of honesty, be honest. If you want a world of justice, be just. If you want a world of love, then love.*

This then is followed by short descriptions of student upsets around the world, beginning with the one which presumably started it all, at Berkeley, and ending with a panoramic view of America in 1969, reviewing once again the full catalog of social ills against which presumably the students are moving. The thing which intrigues in this collection of student writing is just how pompous student statements really are. Thus the University of California at Berkeley is described as in a state of siege. From West Germany comes this claim: "Youth is unmasking the pomp and circumstance of academic ceremonies with the slogan 'Under the robes and gowns is the mold of a thousand years.'" And from Paris came the much-quoted remark, "A spectre is haunting Europe—the spectre of student revolt." However, the reader who perseveres beyond the rhetoric of these essays can find common strands in all nations. Institutions have grown too rapidly, have become too complex, and have tried to assimilate too heterogeneous student bodies without the requisite instrumentalities. As either the pace of expansion slows or as better instruments for selection of students are created, student activism very likely will ease. Perhaps if student activities have contributed to this slowing down process, maybe their efforts are not completely in vain.

E. J. Kahn, Jr.
HARVARD: THROUGH CHANGE AND THROUGH STORM
New York: Norton, 1969

The author, a Harvard graduate, spent a year on the Harvard campus and was there during the time of the occupation of the administration building and the calling of police. This is a well-written but fluffy interpretation. What emerges is an almost precious adoration of Harvard as the greatest of American collegiate institutions. It, according to the author, almost has a corner on the market for outstanding academicians. Its students are the brightest and its contributions to the nation are the greatest. He devotes full chapters to such things as the admissions process and how the university goes about obtaining its carefully screened classes, to the contributions which Harvard made to the federal government, especially during the Kennedy administration, and to life in the residence hall. If one examines the book carefully, there is considerable information about Harvard and most of it seems reasonably accurate. However, the romanticizing quality of the entire treatment makes it suspect as an important piece of reporting about that university. Hence the book will find its best audience among the alumni.

Robert Kavanaugh
THE GRIM GENERATION
New York: Trident Press, 1970

Kavanaugh has written what is almost a mood poem, full of apt but somewhat stereotypic observations. The author is far from critical of the young, seeing that in spite of error they might finally convert university campuses into democratic institutions; and he finds much in the way campuses have operated to stimulate a revolutionary fervor. But as part of this laudable effort, students lost their sense of humor. He sees much of the college population as a kept generation, having generally more of everything than they really need. Students realize this status. Most would like to be on their own but only a few take such irrevocable steps as joining the Peace Corps or Vista. The genuine hippies within the college community are not unlike the earlier saints who believed that fasting, preaching, self-flagellation were essential to salvation. So many of the young, the author believes, are part of a graveyard generation in which a real zest for living has disappeared, as in one way or another they opt out of the human struggle.

> *This generation of students is deathly serious. The dreamers seem willing to fight and maybe even to die, not in Vietnam, but to ameliorate the wrongs of our world. The campus is the testing ground, the place where America will find, if she is able to change, in the face of social upheaval, to meet the demands of new problems. Lovers of the university system in America must feel like crying when they see the campus become another Coliseum where students are thrown to hungry lions for the quick satisfaction of those who require easy answers.*

In the end, the author makes some prescriptions, including elimination of parental service to youth, search for a revitalized sense of humor, and, above all, a return of effective professors to the university campus. He sees much of student grimness as questing for the intellectual help which great college teachers presumably once gave. "Never have we so needed the return of a venerable Mr. Chips to our academic institutions."

J. Frank Ligon, ed.
CONFRONTATIONS
Corvallis: Oregon State University Press, 1970

Campus Unrest

This book contains the Proceedings of the Thirty-First Annual Pacific Northwest Conference on Higher Education and is quite unusual among conference proceedings in that it actually presents exchanges of opinion from the discussion sessions and in a sufficiently continuous way to make a readable document. The overall theme stresses three elements, although they are not treated discretely in time. The first concerns black expectations and institutional response; the second, larger causes for campus unrest; and the third, the facts and implications of confrontation as an emerging way of academic life. The papers and discussions by both black and white participants reflect approval of black studies, approval of black demands, and a quest for understanding of student dissent and even confrontation. A number of the remarks reflected the nostra culpa strain, although a few speakers did suggest that the university did not present a completely bad record in responding to student rights and demands and in dealing with black students. The thesis is never explicitly stated, yet there seemed to be an undertone to the entire conference approving a radical shift in posture to allow the university to become much more active in political and social causes. As one of the principal speakers opined, three options seemed currently available: maintenance of the status quo, closing the institution down, or rapid evolution of the university to the point where it must deal actively with radically different social problems. As a document to be read, this set of conference proceedings would have been improved had there been sharper differences reflected in some of the papers. However, as a conference, the blander, more homogeneous libertarianism probably was a good thing, given the potentially explosive quality of the subjects.

David C. Nichols
PERSPECTIVES ON CAMPUS TENSIONS
Washington: American Council on Education, 1970

This collection of papers was for the most part prepared specifically for the American Council on Education to help educators understand campus unrest. Some represent fresh views, as does "Presidential Discontent," or Bolding's "Fundamental Considerations." However, Lipset and Keniston seem to be saying here what they have said in many other places. Overall, the collection should be of considerable help.

David C. Nichols, Olive Mills, eds.
THE CAMPUS CRISIS
Washington: American Council on Education, 1970

This book presents the papers and discussion at the annual conference of the American Council on Education held in October, 1969. As has been true in the past several years, the proceedings comprise several commissioned papers designed to present the issue and the shorter papers of commentary delivered at the conference itself. Generally, the papers reflect a middle ground regarding the racial crisis rather than the real national polarity of opinion. Thus, one of the Negro speakers was almost antagonistic toward black studies, black separatism and the like, finding these did not attack the central problem of bringing Negro leadership into the existing large corporate educational and governmental structures. And that position was joined by a white commentator sharply critical of excesses in black studies and calling for application to them of the same criteria applied to other academic efforts. Other papers ranged slightly to the left or right of these positions, but none expressed forcefully the argument for black separatism nor forcefully the argument for maintaining traditional ways of institutional functioning. Perhaps the most radical suggestion concerned open admissions, bringing into question the orthodox approaches to admittance through academic aptitude and established gradepoint averages. This collection of reasonably well written and argued presentations may receive the same criticism which John Munro leveled at one of the prepared papers. Said he, "It was too cool"; it apparently didn't sense the urgency of the racial issue on the nation's campuses. The reader will obtain a number of ideas for dealing with the racial issue on campuses but will find little in the way of validated or proven practices—probably such knowledge is as yet unavailable. Five years from now there should be a much more solid base of evidence on which to conduct discussion. But in faltering ways this collection of papers does begin to elaborate the thesis that blacks and whites in the United States do see things substantially differently, and that much greater use must be made of black vision in the future if significant improvement is to be brought about.

William R. Rogers
THE ALIENATED STUDENT
Nashville, Tenn.: Board of Education, United Methodist Church, 1969

This small book is a reasonably accurate quick review of conventional interpretations of today's college students. The author feels that alienated young people are concerned about deep and complex moral issues and that problems on campus are rooted in moral perplexities. He recognizes several different sorts of alienation: an extreme almost psychotic form, dropping out of the mainstream to join a subculture, political alienation, and revolt against the social and civil injustices contemporary society inflicts. Much of the alienation is sparked by the ugliness, stupidity and arrogance of American policy in Vietnam and by the technological dehumanization in American culture. Much of what we see on the campus is the students' desperate struggle to recover the humanizing element. But students also seem to be protesting the over-reliance on scientific positivism and are searching for ways actually to deal with the evil which the scientist tends to ignore. Of course, many other factors are involved. The credit mentality seems to frighten students who don't want to find themselves chained down to a load of monthly bills, and this may be a factor in students' deferring commitment. The destruction of the environment, affluence and the mass media are also seen as directly involved. Perhaps the biggest weakness of this short book is the lack of any historical perspective against which to compare current versions of student alienation. The big virtue is, of course, a short, concise presentation of conventional liberal wisdom as to what has caused student unrest.

Edward E. Sampson, Harold A. Korn, eds.
STUDENT ACTIVISM AND PROTEST
San Francisco: Jossey-Bass, 1970

This collection of presumably research-based essays which still contain impressive amounts of speculation and polemic is highly consistent with the "liberal," "developmental," "understanding" school of commentators about the affairs of youth. These essays reveal a by now well known profile of protesting and dissenting youth. They are seen generally as intelligent, able, self-actualizing individuals coming from homes which, while not free from tension, encouraged and supported questioning attitudes toward a variety of social issues. Within the broad category of dissenting youth, of course, several sub-categories are recognized and some differentiation is made, say, between dissenting youth and alienated youth and between protesting youth and those involved in a definite strike, but all of the readily perceivable sub-categories have neither been listed nor elaborated.

Similarly, the forces and factors presented here as contributing to the outbreak of student activism in the late 1960s have also received wide currency elsewhere. Thus, mass education at large, impersonal campuses looms large, as does general disenchantment with the most visible malfunctionings of American democracy. Much of the early protest activity was associated with the civil rights movement and then gradually drifted to a preoccupation with the war in Vietnam and its various correlates. The impact of the technology, the possible generation gap, and unaccounted for distance between social values and values acquired in the home are all presented in one way or another. And in general this humane developmental point of view is one which I personally tend to support.

However, some questions intrude which properly should be explored before definitive statements can be made. Several of the essays use as proof of the general healthfulness of dissenting youth psychometrically derived categories based on somewhat loaded questions. Thus, openness to new experience is ultimately defined by how students respond to statements prepared by a test writer who believes he knows what openness really is. No attempt has been made to test how the more and the less valued traits actually serve an individual subsequently in his life development. In a concluding chapter a few follow-up studies are presented but in a somewhat unsatisfactory way. Generally these writers seem to be pleading for youth and urging a greater understanding of the problems young people face. They seem to accept as valid the objects about which students complain without attending to the truly vast changes in higher education which were well underway even before the outbreaks of student protest. Similarly, should there not be a more careful assessment of the actual outcomes of student protest? In such a book written for publication in 1970 one also wonders why the political implications of student protest were not examined in considerable detail. If the general impact of idealized aspirations is hurtful, should not the amount and kind of hurt be presented? Then, too, should not greater attention be paid to historical settings and historical parallels? The writers come for the most part from the social and behavioral sciences and seem with rare exceptions to be oblivious to historical and even economic patterns.

There are critics and observers of the current educational scene whose judgments are respected and whose perceptions are likely to be considerably different from those contained in the Sampson, Korn book. The names of Russell Kirk, Sidney Hook or Charles Frankel come quickly to mind. One wonders what interpretations these men would make of the same data for some sort of idealized future and definitive interpretation of the events of the late 1960s. It is interesting to dream of subjecting the same data to men and women of many different persuasions in an effort finally to arrive at something approximating truth.

These remarks may sound unnecessarily critical. If they do, this is indeed unfortunate. Those who prepared the essays are thoughtful and respected scholars and they have striven mightily to understand. If their understandings seem deficient it is probably only because sufficient time has not elapsed to allow historical perspective.

Robert Smith, Richard Axen, DeVere Pentony
BY ANY MEANS NECESSARY
San Francisco: Jossey-Bass, 1970

These active participants attempt to explain the events leading up to and characterizing student and faculty unrest on the San Francisco State campus in the late 1960s. The treatment is basically chronological, showing briefly how San Francisco State changed from a good teachers college into a large liberal urban state college within a decade. Then, following on the heels of the campus upsets at the University of California in 1964, the institution moved from one crisis to another until it was virtually immobilized as a result of the student and faculty strike. Several themes run through the interpretation. The first is that liberal student leaders became the victims of radical students who wished to use the inertia of experimental college thinking to restructure the entire college and possibly go on from there to structure the entire university. The radical cause was given material by pressures from the Third World Community in San Francisco for greater servicing of their needs, and by the increasing hostility toward the war in Vietnam, the military, and any war-related activities. People figure largely in this interpretation, with a liberal young president, John Summerskill, shown as being completely inadequate to cope with the revolutionary forces, pressured as he was by the board of trustees, the public press, radical students, faculty and key administrative associates, each having a different vision of what was taking place. Glenn Dumke, the chancellor of the state college system, is another negative but influential individual whose tendency either to go with or placate conservative members of the board of trustees tended at almost every point to undercut efforts to keep San Francisco State functioning and its various radical elements under control. George Murray, a militant black professor, occupies another distinct position as he almost singlehandedly alienated conservative and middle-class elements in the state who, to get at him, limited San Francisco State at every turn. On one occasion he delivered a violent speech at Fresno which, when reported to the board of trustees then in session, seems to have caused a decision against building a new student union. Next to Dumke and Murray, the faculty of San Francisco State emerges as lacking in creativity but having enormous aptitude for muddying the water and placing the administration in untenable positions. One of the authors was president of San Francisco State following John Summerskill and he describes in considerable detail the steps he took to administer the institution, keep it cool and generate some of the necessary extra funding needed if such things as the demands of Third World students were to be met. At each step along the way he lost more and more support, which never was more than lukewarm. Smith finally resigned, explaining, "The blunt fact was that I quit as president mainly, but not exclusively, because we failed in six months of strenuous effort on the part of my administrative staff and me, to get from the chancellor and the trustees the resources and the kinds of decisions I felt we needed if we were to dig the college out of the institutional debris which my administration inherited." His resignation was followed by the student-faculty strike, characterized by episodes of bloody confrontation with police, and then the appointment of president Hayakawa as acting president, ending the strike and bringing quiet, which has now lasted almost eighteen months, to San Francisco State. By the end, the college had become a major political issue. This is an amazingly well written document. It probably will not make radical students happy, nor will it make Chancellor Dumke particularly happy; but as compared with other attempts to interpret San Francisco State, it seems by far the most thorough, scholarly, and objective work available.

Richard Zorza
THE RIGHT TO SAY WE
New York: Praeger, 1970

The Literature of Higher Education 1971

This young British student has added one more to an already overburdened list of student-impressionistic interpretations of campus revolt. He presents his reactions to seeing Harvard University torn apart by student upheaval. He came to Harvard, one guesses, with high hopes and aspirations and found that attending college can be a lonely, disagreeable and disillusioning experience. The fact that it has also been so to previous generations doesn't seem to occur to him. There apparently was considerable student disenchantment with life at Harvard, but the real stimulators of student outbreak were the war in Vietnam, the draft, and ROTC on the campus. Once the administration building was occupied, student interest began to boil; and once the administration called the police to clear the building, a wild sense of frustration pervaded the atmosphere. This young author is quite perceptive in describing his own feelings and those of other students about such events as police on campus, but nowhere does he attempt to empathize with those who were really responsible for the continuation of the university. The hyperbole which characterizes his analysis throughout is the hyperbole of excited youth. For example:

> *As an institution the university has totally abdicated the responsibility that once gave it a useful place in society. It has degenerated into a billion dollar conglomerate which provides a quiet and lucrative environment for the social scientist who often has not the courage to face the real world, a research and resource center for the physical scientist who will sell his services to the highest bidder, an apprentice shop for those who need some smattering and understanding of the world before they can fit into their unfulfilling lives.*

As one-sided grist for some future historical interpretation of the '60s the book has some merit, just as the various national white papers on the outbreak of World War I had some merit. But it is fundamentally an emotional brief for only one side of a highly complicated set of issues.

Six

REFLECTIONS

Some of these are good, others less so, but none seems of major lasting quality, partly one suspects because they all must be topical enough to meet the authors' other purposes.

Robert F. Goheen
THE HUMAN NATURE OF A UNIVERSITY
Princeton, N.J.: Princeton University Press, 1969

This book is a distillation of ideas contained in speeches, reports, and other papers prepared by President Goheen during his twelve years at Princeton. The slim volume reveals much about the author, who sees that a basic commitment to the life of the mind most properly characterizes the university and can best be pursued in a reasonably tranquil atmosphere. Not that tensions can ever be obliterated, but too much tension and conflict can destroy the fundamental nature of a university. The author feels that the modern university is intimately involved in contriving the survival of civilization and the future of the human race. And this, because of the complexity of human issues, should force the university's attention to matters close to home. However, the university must guard itself against too precipitous and direct involvement in events and seek more pervasive ways of insuring survival. Thus, while President Goheen searches for a balance between detachment and involvement, the fact that he is by training a classicist inclines him more toward detachment which allows for reflection. Although the book is small, and the author clearly does not attempt to deal intensively with all of the problems of higher education, the book does touch on most of the significant ones and brings an idealistic quality to bear which is exceedingly refreshing and hopeful. For example, toward the end of the book the author recognizes the complexity of problems but suggests that they should be approached with courage even to produce but small solutions.

Samuel E. Gould
TODAY'S ACADEMIC CONDITION
New York: McGraw-Hill, 1970

Gould here reveals once again that he is one of the more thoughtful observers of the current educational scene. He develops these essays as part of a symposium conducted by Colgate University, and one gets the impression from internal evidence that he would like this book to stand as the author's educational credo. He feels, as do others, that the university has never been more necessary to the national life but never in a more precarious position. If the university is to survive, it must come to terms realistically with its traditional commitment to the democratic ideal in education. It has long

Reflections

preached but long failed to practice democracy. Thus it must really come to grips with such problems as how to achieve universal higher education in a nation where the educational channels are already clogged and congested. Issue after issue reveals a fundamental dilemma of the American university. If it takes the position that a decent regard should be shown for the opinions of mankind, it stands accused of cowardice and collaboration with regressive forces in the society. However, if it takes a position that any word is free to be spoken, it is accused of fomenting rebellion. The university has obviously been confronted by a host of demands. However, it has still not been confounded by them. It will be confounded, however, unless it as an institution takes the initiative in reconsidering its place in society.

As the university ponders its role, it should at least acknowledge some of the very real glories which it has achieved. For example, although inequities abound, the United States has roughly ten per cent of its Negroes attending college, a percentage as large as the number of European whites who attend. And there are other glories. However, there are weaknesses also—dreariness and pedantry in many of the courses; the university's failure to recognize just how much education is going on outside institutional walls. As these and other matters are considered, it should be possible to dream of the future. The university can neither tolerate a revolution nor remain conservative; but Gould believes the university will reform itself through evolutionary processes. New sorts of objectives for the institution will be created. The institution will relate much more closely to developments off campus. The present departmental arrangement will probably eventually be judged obsolete and replaced by something else. The electronic revolution must finally make its way onto the campus. Governance will be provided which at once will restore needed power to central officers and yet provide ways for more general participation in government.

The university of the future, as I envision it, will be a loose federation of all the educational and cultural forces of a community at every age level. It will be a coordinated educational entity serving a single, fairly large community or a single compact region. If a group of communities is more important, whether it will have a single name, or even be called a university any longer is hard to say. Parts of it will undoubtedly have names similar to those they do now, but what we think of today as the college or the university will constitute only a portion of the future role.

This is a perceptive book, an idealistic book, and a needed book. Faculties may be more intransigent than even Gould can dream.

Algo D. Henderson
THE INNOVATIVE SPIRIT
San Francisco: Jossey-Bass, 1970

Henderson has written almost a personal philosophy of education. Putting together his long experience as dean and president at Antioch, and his years spent examining various facets of higher education, he comes out with a generally liberal and reforming document, tempered with evidence of the difference between ideals and reality. He clearly sees higher education as a reflection of a democratic ideology and views education as a means of making essential changes in the society. Thus he clearly rejects the idea of a university as an ivory tower. His concepts of the processes of education seem quite pragmatic as he searches for ways to provide experiences for students through which they grow and mature. Henderson ponders the newer instrumentalities available to higher education. He seems generally supportive of systems of institutions, community colleges, reality-based education, reforms in the status of students, and a collegial system of governance. A weakness in the book is that he doesn't seem sharply enough critical of some of the very real failures of these innovations. But perhaps this is not really a weakness. There may have been too much apocalyptic writing, hence a humane optimism may be desirable at the present. It is difficult to place this book accurately among contributions to the literature of higher education. It is not polemical writing. Although the author deeply believes some of the things he says, it is neither a sociological nor psychological tract, nor is it contemporary history. Rather, it is an extended and thoughtful essay reflective more of opinion than firmly established fact. Reading the book straight through would prove burdensome; but selecting essays at random is a rewarding experience.

Francis H. Horn
CHALLENGE AND PERSPECTIVE IN HIGHER EDUCATION
Carbondale: Southern Illinois University Press, 1971

The author has brought together some of his public speeches delivered on a number of different occasions: inaugurations, graduations and professional conferences. They reveal the author to be broadly knowledgeable about higher education and reasonably sophisticated in relating education to other strands in American culture. He sees as the major problems standing in the way of a better world for all people the population explosion, ethnic, racial and religious prejudice, and the threat of war. And contrary to considerable contemporary thinking, he is basically optimistic that these problems can be solved. But they won't be solved if educators persist in an unrealistic quest for some idealized version of liberal education. Not that he is against the liberal arts and sciences, but he believes also in vocational preparation and a real-life application of the liberal arts and sciences. He particularly would like to have college professors get out of their ivory towers and learn at first hand the realities of all phases of life in twentieth century America. But he is no social actionist for institutions themselves. He views their primary responsibilities as educative and points out that they weaken themselves fundamentally as they disperse too many resources to such things as preoccupation with research. If institutions are to occupy themselves properly, strong presidential leadership will be the first requirement. While there are some who believe that the presidency currently is an untenable position, Horn's judgment appears to be otherwise. Throughout the book, Horn, in much more charitable language than I would use, holds up to scrutiny items of contemporary belief or mythology. Thus he recognizes that institutional research is valuable but is far from a panacea. He is persuaded that the fraternities, if their abuses could be corrected, come close to being the ideal for which a number of activist students are searching. And he is clearly not an apologist for youth. He is quite willing to say that many in the older generation, including himself, are not nearly as obtuse or as bad as young radical students claim. Having followed Horn's career for some time, I welcome this collection but would like to have seen him include some of his other published work, such as a few of his book reviews, so that the broader dimensions of his thinking about higher education could have been exposed.

Edward H. Levi
POINT OF VIEW
Chicago: University of Chicago Press, 1969

This is a collection of speeches and papers prepared by the president of the University of Chicago. They deal with such diverse topics as The University and the Modern Condition; The University and the Profession; or The Role of the University in Liberal Arts Education. The speeches were given between 1963 and 1969 and hence reflect many of the concerns of that period.

Lewis B. Mayhew
ARROGANCE ON CAMPUS
San Francisco: Jossey-Bass, 1970

Some of the author's friends contend this book is an autobiographical statement—and it may be. The book reflects on

Reflections

campus unrest during the last half of the 1960s to find out why turmoil happened and what the prognosis is likely to be. The author feels that large size, rapid change and frequent administrative ineptness set a stage on which arrogance of faculty members and arrogance of students could collide. While the reasons for some of the aberrant professorial and student behavior can be found, nonetheless each group is responsible for changes more frequently hurtful than helpful. The author does not feel that students have much of a role in governance, nor does he believe that faculties, as presently organized, are likely to govern responsibly. The results of conflict on campus are several. Loss of support from the larger public seems the first outcome with the possible serious modification of such values as academic freedom being a likely next outcome. The concluding chapter in the book was written after the events of April and May 1970, including the Cambodian, Kent State and Jackson State uprisings. The author sees those three episodes as being qualitatively different from earlier ones. Largely as a result of those episodes, however, he anticipates a steady diminishing of tension on campuses. Those events seem to have forced college students and their professors to a precipice, and they didn't like what they saw below. Hence, after May 1970, there was a general stepping back from all confrontation and that withdrawal continued into late 1970. Both the author and the reviewer hope this will be the last book for some time to come which the author must write to interpret campus turmoil.

Paul C. Reinert, ed.
THE URBAN CATHOLIC UNIVERSITY
New York: Sheed & Ward, 1970

Reinert has collected a number of speeches given over the last twenty years. Generally, they reveal a combination of idealism, practical experience, and a firm belief in a number of principles said to be characteristic of American democracy. He recognizes the problems of Catholic higher education but insists on unique objectives and unique ways of achieving those which should allow Catholic higher education to remain viable. He sees particularly that Catholic institutions located in urban areas have even more special problems than other sorts of institutions, but believes it quite appropriate for them to work directly on urban problems. Running throughout many of the essays is his very natural concern with how higher education, particularly the private sector, is to be financed, and what should be the appropriate role for the federal government. Thus he wants to know to what extent colleges and universities should be free to determine their own purposes and objectives in view of federal involvement in finance. He inquires into the age-old distinction between public and private higher education. He ponders the shifting enrollment differentials between the public and the private sector of higher education, and he deals with the issue, although perhaps not head on, of whether the present college generation or the previous one should pay the cost of higher education. The book, as a record of the evolving thoughts of an extraordinarily capable administrator, is of considerable value. By indicating where we have been, the essays may contribute to determining where we should go.

M. A. F. Ritchie
THE COLLEGE PRESIDENCY
New York: Philosophical Library, 1969

In the genre of didactic memoir, Ritchie describes his experiences as president, first at Hardwick College and then at Pacific University. Ritchie tells much about himself and his family and, by implication, the role of the old-time, small liberal arts college president. The centrality of the presidency in the life of the college comes clear, as does the goldfish-bowl style of life which that imposes on the president and his family. The necessity of excellent secretarial help, strong administrative assistance and, of course, good board relationships is stressed, as is the president's ability to relate well with all kinds of constituencies. Ritchie believes that the faculty should have an important voice in institutional concerns. He also

Reflections

believes that presidential prerogatives necessary to govern should not be infringed. One gets the impression that the author has been able to grow with changing times, which includes students and faculty on key committees, but that he would be more comfortable if those developments had not come quite so rapidly. This is not a profound book, nor does the author leap to large generalization and theoretical formulation, yet it is a warmly written book from which one may derive many reasonably validated principles for practice. In a time of apocalyptic writing and rapid turnover among college presidencies, it is heartening to come across a still optimistic book. Ritchie closes his little work with these comments:

> *Shortly after I came to Pacific University, I wrote an article entitled, "I Am Glad To Be A College President." It was published in a national magazine. I wrote it largely because I was somewhat fed up with the complaints of college presidents who were resigning in large numbers and rationalizing their resignations in print. I deliberately emphasized the positive side of the presidency. Now, after having been President at two institutions for a period of sixteen years, I am asked the question "Are you still glad?" The answer is emphatically "Yes."*

Samuel A. Small
HIGHER EDUCATION IN THE AGE OF SCIENCE
Boston: Christopher, 1970

If the ideas contained in this book were really taken seriously, there would be even greater grounds for student protest than currently exist. The tone of the book is exemplified by a sentence from the Preface, "Besides tightening up on standards, the crying need of the American college today is to eliminate superfluous courses that are taught for the local convenience of industrial companies." Thereafter, he goes on to call for the purity of the liberal arts, a centralized national system of education, a generally prescribed curriculum (even no participation in extracurricular activities during the freshman year), using marks and classroom responses to be sure that only the best survive, an education designed to develop the highest virtue—which the author considers to be a love of reading—and a style of teaching which "brings about the emergence of good taste and the moral tone which students inevitably feel if the teacher has any depth of character." The author feels that since science dominates American life, science should dominate the college curriculum. He seems to favor required chapel attendance, mental discipline, and precise training in English. The virtue of the book is that it probably will be little read and of no influence. The author reveals himself to be a far too typical English professor, governing his life—and, he hopes, the lives of his students —by ideology long since past.

Robert E. Strain
THE RELEVANT PROFESSOR
Orange, Calif.: Polaris, 1970

This stupid little book is an autobiographical statement of a professor of economics at one of the California state colleges who disliked some actions of his more liberal colleagues and campaigned assiduously through Letters to the Editor and other communications on these matters. Now there is nothing wrong in this sort of thing, but does the literature of higher education need to be cluttered with a resumé of these efforts? But at least the author will have a book on his official bibliography.

Seven

INSTITUTIONAL DIFFERENCES

These seem so much better than the purely descriptive ones of years past. For the most part, using of course different techniques, they reflect a growing desire to base generalizations on research-generated evidence. And Dunham's book did win the American Council on Education's annual Bordens Book Award.

Burton R. Clark
THE DISTINCTIVE COLLEGE
Chicago: Aldine, 1970

The Literature of Higher Education 1971

Clark has attempted to use sociological theory to uncover the wellsprings of three quite distinctive institutions. He examines Antioch, Reed, and Swarthmore to find out how they became unique and why their distinctiveness has persisted over generations while other colleges in substantially the same starting condition have never thus far emerged. He finds that these three developed, from somewhat different sets of circumstances—Antioch near bankruptcy, Reed newly born, and Swarthmore highly successful and stable but ready to change—what Clark calls a saga, a consistent, sustaining set of myths and cultural norms which are so generally satisfying to present and future clientele that the saga persists. The classic case seems to be Antioch, which was church-related, located in an intellectual and economic cul de sac and unable to attract enough students to keep its doors open. A person with an educational ideal was appointed as president; he quickly sensed the need to change the composition of the board of trustees and attract faculty members who shared his ideal and would take vigorous steps to implant his ideal deeply enough to survive his own departure. The keystone of Arthur Morgan's ideal was, of course, the cooperative work-study program, and he was able to find a large enough number of younger people to work at the scheme and develop an institutionalized system which persisted. In all three institutions strong leadership was apparent. However, while Clark accepts the necessity for strong leadership he adds other elements to the equation. At this point the treatment becomes somewhat loose. Generally, one gets the impression that Clark thinks the concept of saga is a good thing. However, he has exemplified it only with three institutions generally approved by the liberal educational conventional wisdom. One wishes Clark had included such institutions as Bob Jones or Wheaton College, which have also developed a consistent ethos extending over time but with quite different educational and social results. However, the book is a distinct contribution, made more valuable by the fact that its general findings are consistent with other studies of innovation, such as Hefferlin's book or Warren Bryan Martin's *Conformity*. What next should be done, of course, is for practitioners of some of the private institutions now struggling for existence to assimilate the principles from Clark's book to see whether or not distinctive colleges can still be created. It may be that Clark insufficiently weighed broad social and economic forces which made the development of a saga possible in one generation and impossible to recreate in another.

E. Alden Dunham
COLLEGES OF THE FORGOTTEN AMERICANS
New York: McGraw-Hill, 1969

At the request of the Carnegie Commission on Higher Education, the author visited a number of somewhat casually selected state colleges and state universities and presents a panoramic view of these. For the most part, these institutions started as normal schools, became teachers colleges, then gradually changed to state colleges, and in some cases have now emerged as regional universities which provide comprehensive programs, although still substantially preoccupied with teacher education. From these institutions come a good cross section of what is probably "the silent majority," young men and women who wish to be trained for jobs which will represent upward social mobility. They have, until recently, been taught by those who were primarily concerned with teaching and had little interest or inclination toward research. While there are differences—for example, some state colleges still emphasize teacher preparation and apparently have no aspirations for graduate work and research—the more general pattern is for these state colleges to work toward some version of full university status. As this striving progresses, the proportion of faculty holding PhD's increases. Presidents come more and more from the PhD rather than from the EdD ranks, and faculties quest for lower teaching loads and greater opportunities to do research. The author seeks to channel the pattern in what he considers more healthy directions for growth. He is sharply critical of the orthodox PhD, and believes that the time is now ripe for the creation of a teaching doctorate which will prepare people for the role of teaching in undergraduate institutions. He believes that the PhD is so firmly entrenched in major universities that change is not likely to happen; but he does believe that the surge to enter graduate work in the state colleges could be directed so as to produce a viable teaching degree. In a sense the book is written to lead up to this central thesis, and the book is likely to be judged by whether or not the thesis is achieved. Earlier, Oliver C. Carmichael wrote a similar book on graduate education, with a similar purpose in mind. His goal was not achieved, and Bernard Berelson's book on graduate education is currently the most frequently cited. As for the methodology of the book, it is clearly soft but probably the most appropriate for the sort of subject studied. The author is knowledgeable and for the most part his insights seem apt. However, some of his generalizations might have been tempered had he had more intimate knowledge of private liberal arts colleges in the Middle West. For example, he frequently compares the state colleges with the Ivy League sort of school, as though these were the two principal types in higher education. The mode of presentation—case study material, some statistics, impressionistic generalization—provides a good variety, and the whole is presented in reasonably felicitous phrasing. If subsequent reports from the Carnegie Commission are of this level, much good will have been done.

Jerry G. Gaff and Associates
THE CLUSTER COLLEGE
San Francisco: Jossey-Bass, 1970

One of the most popular ideas of the reforming fronts in higher education is the cluster college, and the authors have codified much of what is known about this entity. In usually well written chapters, the cluster college is described as dealing with the large size of contemporary institutions, providing a vehicle by which the power of peer interaction can be channeled for educational purposes, and as a device by which faculty and students can convert themselves into a learning team. Most of the better known experi-

Institutional Differences

ments with cluster colleges are discussed in some detail, running from the several conceptualized in the mid-1950s, such as Hofstra College and Monteith, to the more recently emerging ones of Santa Cruz, University of the Pacific, and Old Westbury. Seeking to go beyond the simple claims of those who created cluster colleges, several chapters of research findings are presented. These support the overly simplified generalization that cluster colleges did attract a somewhat different kind of student than did the larger configurations but show the cluster college did make a more significant impact on those students. While this is as complete a treatment of cluster colleges as can be found, nonetheless several omissions are serious enough for attention. The authors at no time discuss seriously enough the financial implications of cluster colleges. Yet, until the economic problems are solved, cluster colleges seem likely to remain interesting but somewhat discrete experiments. Nor do the authors deal with the knotty problem of faculty and how one harnesses loyalties of faculty members in large research-oriented universities for a sustained period of time, given the continued presence of departments oriented toward graduate study and research. Thirdly, it does not appear that the authors seriously questioned the applicability of the cluster college idea to different sorts of institutions. It would have been helpful, for example, to have some elaboration and critical analysis of the several commuting junior colleges which have tried to develop cluster colleges. Overall, however, the book is so outstanding compared with the bulk of published literature concerning higher education that it deserves wide reading and serious discussion on the part of all of those concerned with undergraduate collegiate education.

Andrew M. Greeley
FROM BACKWATER TO MAINSTREAM
New York: McGraw-Hill, 1969

The author pulls together his impressions about Catholic higher education and in a concise way adequately portrays the

The Literature of Higher Education 1971

emerging picture. Catholic higher education, originally created to achieve parochial and religious ends, is now merging into the mainstream following almost exactly patterns created by other forms of denominational and secular institutions. He points out that Catholic higher education is far from a monolith reflecting; there is just about as great diversity within the Catholic orbit as in higher education generally. There are weak, struggling institutions of small size and limited faculty on the one hand, and on the other comprehensive universities such as Notre Dame which stand on the threshold of greatness in education. At the time the book was written he did not feel that any Catholic institution had achieved stature of first rank; but he feels that Notre Dame is quite likely to make that achievement. He argues that as Notre Dame goes so will likely go the rest of Catholic higher education in America. At the end of his resumé he points out the numerous and for the most part quite obvious problems which perplex Catholic higher education. Almost all have lived in the past on tuition and contributed services of religious, both of which sources are now being limited. Fund-raising has not been particularly successful in the past, but fund-raising may be one of the more helpful devices for balancing budgets in the future. On the whole, Catholic institutions face a rather grim financial future; but some of them at least are making the difficult choices in order to survive economically. Perhaps the only major caveat which this reader would make is a difference in judgment about several individual institutions. I share his enthusiasm for Notre Dame and for Immaculate Heart; but several others which I have examined firsthand I find less responsive than does he. Father Greeley's instructions in preparing the book were to synthesize and bring up to date work he had published elsewhere. This he has done in readable and thoughtful style, and the job need not be redone for at least half a decade.

Harold L. Hodgkinson
INSTITUTIONS IN TRANSITION
Berkeley, Calif.: The Carnegie Commission on Higher Education, 1970

Institutional Differences

In about 1965, Mayhew observed in his book on American higher education that colleges and universities seemed to be regressing toward a mean form whether the institution started off as a technical school, a liberal arts college, a private institution, or whatever. The observation was based on qualitative evidence which has now been validated by quantitative evidence. Hodgkinson documents that institutions of various sorts are changing in substantially the same direction. While diversity of higher education to serve a pluralistic society is the ideal cited constantly in speeches and polemics, the actual situation is a steady drift toward homogeneity. Hodgkinson also documents that in spite of claims made or expressed desires for smaller institutions, size is the most important single factor in determining institutional growth and in determining institutional rate of change. In effect, the big places get bigger faster and the big places make the most changes in response to changing social conditions. The empirical demonstration of these facts is so important that it is a shame the book was not put out in a more permanent form and through a medium likely to gain it more attention. Many of the Carnegie Commission's works are being published and, hopefully, being publicized by McGraw-Hill. Why this one was handled by the Commission itself and distributed through its Berkeley offices is nowhere indicated. The survey and sampling were excellently done and one can only hope that a revised version will come out soon to be more widely read.

William A. Hoppe, ed.
POLICIES AND PRACTICES IN EVENING COLLEGES, 1969
Metuchen, N.J.: Scarecrow Press, 1969

Here is simply a highly factual reporting on an elaborate questionnaire study of institutions offering evening work through colleges and divisions. A total of 107 institutions responded and their answers suggest some general tendencies. Most institutions have flexible admissions policies for adults, with no particular deadline for applications. A majority allow adults to register for credit courses without submitting a transcript, and a large majority allow adults as special or non-degree students. Almost half of the institutions are engaged in correspondence courses, and three-quarters of them allow students to take credit courses without examination. Only a minority offer special degree programs for adults but an equal number are considering offering special degree programs. About half charge lower fees for evening students and a majority have no fixed policies regarding use of part- or full-time faculty. Deans or directors just about as frequently as departments have responsibility for hiring full-time faculty for evening classes. There is some research going on concerning adult education and a minority of institutions are now using students to discuss curricular matters. Three-quarters of the institutions seem to receive adequate support from central administration. This obviously is not a book one uses for bedtime reading but it does present useful information, institution by institution, on the matters covered by the questionnaire. It's not likely that a movie will be made on the basis of this.

Neil G. McCluskey, ed.
THE CATHOLIC UNIVERSITY: A MODERN APPRAISAL
Notre Dame: University of Notre Dame Press, 1970

Father McCluskey presents a number of essays prepared by thoughtful men about the nature of Catholic higher education, its uniquenesses and its relationship to the rest of American higher education. It is a document clearly in the mainstream of modernizing the Catholic Church. The framework for the collection is provided by an approving discussion of what came to be called the Land O'Lakes statement, which demanded that the Catholic university must be a university in the full sense of the word, willing and able to be independent of strictures which church hierarchy in the past may have imposed. The writers generally reach the conclusion that there is an important place in the modern world for Catholic institutions of higher education which can express, exemplify and value Catholicity and still maintain academic freedom in all fields in its purest sense. Father Andrew Greeley, for example, argues that there properly is no difference between academic freedom in a Catholic institution and academic freedom in a secular one. Father Theodore Hesburgh perhaps caught the total spirit of the book in his introduction:

> *Our central role in the modern world is to be among the best of universities in the full meaning of the word, and to be Catholic in the full contemporary sweep of the Church's concern for worldwide human development, in its ultimate personal, social, cultural, spiritual, and even material dimensions. One need only scan the long list of human problematics in Vatican Council II's Constitution on The Chuch in the Modern World to perceive the magnitude of our task.*

David Riesman, Joseph Gusfield, Zelda Gamson
ACADEMIC VALUES AND MASS EDUCATION
New York: Doubleday, 1970

The title may be somewhat presumptuous for essentially the book presents two detailed case studies of somewhat atypical institutions. It compares the evolution of Michigan State University, Oakland, with the development of Monteith College, which was created and has been maintained as an experimental alternative for the complex, urban-based Wayne University in Detroit. The principal mode of study consisted of detailed interviewing of people on the two campuses, visiting classes, and studying other records such as any accreditation team might use. Their impressions are placed in a national context which has seen an enormous expansion in higher education as an enterprise and a public embrace of the concept of universal higher education. The authors alternate between chapters devoted to one of the institutions and chapters treating observations and principles derived from both. Thus, the creation of the Oakland campus in the Detroit area is described as a move by Michigan State University to obtain political influence in that populous portion of the state. The move was made possible in spite of a policy statement against branch campuses by the receipt of a substantial gift of land and money for the creation of a branch in that part of the state. It was obvious to many, except to the first recruited faculty, that a state university would attract a distinctive kind of student. When faculty pretensions of academic purity encountered the reality of vocationally oriented students, trouble resulted. Through the particularly adroit leadership of the chancellor, the branch campus corrected abuse and prospered to a point of almost complete autonomy. Monteith campus was organized partly out of some interests of the then-president, partly because of the availability of Ford Foundation money to support studies of new types of institutions, and partly because of the general education interests of some of the faculty members at Wayne State who were freed from teaching to construct an alternative model institution. Each of these institutions tried to create new sorts of curricula; the resulting differences may be attributed to the different prior experiences of the first faculty. Thus, the first faculty at MSU, Oakland, were relatively young discipline-oriented people who saw a new experiment as intriguing but not necessarily determining their full professional careers. Hence, the curriculum had a more disciplinary flavor than that at Monteith where the faculties were older; many of them viewed the Monteith experience as a second career to last until retirement. Thus, at Monteith there were many more staff-taught courses of an interdisciplinary character. In both institutions the significance of central administration emerges. Monteith could not have been created without the interest of the president, who was willing to protect the newly created interdisciplinary effort from the tender mercies of the other schools and departments. MSU, Oakland, could not have prospered and flourished as it did had it not been for the political astuteness of its chancellor. However, neither president seems to have influenced in any sustained fashion curricular development once the selection of key subordinate administrators and faculty had been accomplished. Here the authors' observations are entirely consistent with the experiences of other new institutions. Successful evolution has depended in large part on successful initial appointments. Overall, this book is readable, insightful and, properly viewed, can be usefully didactic. It could have been better had the sample of new institutions been enlarged; but this was clearly beyond the resources available to the three scholars. Perhaps the only item of interpretation about which there could be major quarrel is whether or not American higher education is as pluralistic as the authors imply. They see such efforts as the creation of MSU, Oakland, and Monteith as valuable forces to preserve pluralism but perhaps discount too eagerly the enormous forces for homogenization.

Joe L. Speath, Andrew M. Greeley
RECENT ALUMNI AND HIGHER EDUCATION
New York: McGraw-Hill, 1970

The authors report on a follow-up study of 40,000 graduates of 135 accredited or large colleges and universities of the Class of 1961 seven years later, which was requested by the Carnegie Commission on Higher Education. In a series of well written and reasonably clearly documented chapters, the book produces some significant evidence. The prime values of a college education are connected with its general or liberal educational goals rather than vocational training. However, the way graduates view the goals of higher education depends largely on the life roles alumni have chosen for themselves. Thus career training is endorsed as the primary goal by those for whom specific career training was important. Although the authors do not establish the general cultural level of college graduates, they do show that the relationship between quality of college and reading of graduates is minimal and that women probably really are the culture bearers, for they generally read more and express greater interest in the arts. In retrospect, these alumni value some of their college experience, value the goals of education which educators would also most value, but are somewhat skeptical as to how well colleges have achieved what ought to be their most important objectives. Alumni, had they had their college work to do over again, would have taken more work in the arts and the humanities and are somewhat sympathetic with the desires for reform which dissenting students are currently expressing. For their own children, these alumni wish a college to provide a good general education with appropriate career training being second. Politically, the Class of '61 seems best characterized as moderate with a slight leaning toward the left, and a surprising number (almost half) are willing to give qualified support to faculty militancy. Rather unsurprisingly, graduates of private colleges are more likely than graduates of public colleges to make financial contributions to their alma maters, and their emotional attachment and general affluence are also involved. After having presented their findings, the authors embark on some policy recommendations based in part, but only in part, on their empirical data. They are not in the camp with those who see personality development as a major purpose for collegiate education. They do not deny that developmental needs are important, but believe that colleges should stick to a relatively few things which apparently they can do well. Thus, they would stress the intellectual components, the curriculum, and minimize such things as work-study programs, or the currently popular interim period when students can do their own thing in the inner city or elsewhere. Generally, they end on an optimistic note, recognizing that some reforms are going to fail but that others, such as a return to teaching, seem in full tide.

George G. Stern
PEOPLE IN CONTEXT
New York: Wiley, 1970

In the early 1950s, Stern and Pace began exploring the impact of colleges on students. Together they adopted from Murray the concept of environmental press operating on corresponding personality structures. Over the years they developed a technique for assessing environmental press, called the College Characteristics Index, and struggled to develop a corresponding instrument for personality. That latter effort apparently has yet not succeeded, but the

Institutional Differences

College Characteristics Index has been used extensively and does produce reliable measures of institutional differences. In this technically rich book, Stern describes the theory, the processes of instrumentation, and then presents the results of his many corroborating studies. Overall, he found that colleges differ systematically in the kinds of students they attract, that institutions are perceived as quite different entities by the students who attend them. Thus some institutions are seen by their students as being highly intellectual and concerned with ideas, where others, ostensibly the same, are perceived by students as characterized by vocationalism or a high degree of play and social activity. This work represents social science of a high order and does provide the basis for provocative inferences about the nature of collegiate education. The book, however, is not persuasive that the instrument Stern uses can become a routinely systematic way by which any given institution might study itself. The complexities of the phenomenon, coupled with the complexities of instrumentation and analysis probably will restrict the real utility to professionally and technically qualified research workers. No run-of-the-mill director of institutional research could probably handle the materials.

Eight

✯✯✯✯✯✯✯✯✯✯✯✯✯✯✯

CONFERENCE PROCEEDINGS AND SYMPOSIA

✯✯✯✯✯✯✯✯✯✯✯✯✯✯✯

In a sense books listed under other headings could properly be classified here. However, the others had sufficiently precise themes to justify placing them in different categories. These examples run from the outstanding issues of *Daedalus* and *Current Issues in Higher Education* to collections of the purest banality. Some of the essays concealed under this heading, as for example

Conference Proceedings and Symposia

some of McGrath's work, one wishes could be made more quickly available. For others, and charity demands names be withheld, it is a mercy that they lie forever buried.

CURRENT CAMPUS ISSUES
Cambridge, Mass.: University Consultants, 1969

The Proceedings of the June 1969 Institute on College and University Administration are in soft cover and offset printed, which is a shame, because some of the essays are nowhere else to be found. One doesn't know the reason, but the people preparing the principal papers seem to have taken their task more seriously than in some other contexts. Thus Harris Wofford candidly describes their planning experiences at Old Westbury and how student desire for hegemony finally was handled. While the essays on resource management and financial planning are generalized, they nonetheless seem helpful even to persons long experienced in dealing with such matters. The writers of those papers may be a bit sanguine about future federal support for university activities, but at least they make their assumptions explicit. Possibly because his analysis agrees so completely with my own, Peter Schrag's identification of three periods in public attitude toward higher education since World War II seems especially apt.

Daedalus
RIGHTS AND RESPONSIBILITIES: THE UNIVERSITY'S DILEMMA
Summer 1970

The third in a trilogy developed by the American Academy of Arts and Sciences on the contemporary university is presented. This one continues the high level of discourse which characterized the first two, with the essay by McGeorge Bundy perhaps the most telling. Bundy, describing Harvard in the 1950s, sees an almost idyllic place where faculty and students went about their business according to the best personal criteria they could evolve. But in doing so, the faculty particularly were sowing the seeds for ultimate academic discontent. The great personal freedom which major universities allowed their faculties is not sufficient. Institutions, if they are to place their houses in order, must now require a new level of responsible participation in the life of the institution as a whole. "Excellence that does not connect itself to the concerns of others is no longer good enough."

Walter Metzger also contributes a delightful, almost poetical essay in which he first points out some interesting parallels between the student unrest of the sixties and the Protestant Revolt and also suggests the need for rearranging roles within the university. Dissident students no longer seem willing to accept dysjunction in role, by which Metzger means inequality within the institutional context. Substantively, Metzger's best contribution in his long essay is some insight into the events of the Columbia University outbreak in which he participated as one of the deviating faculty members. The overall assessment of this collection is outstanding. The treatment might have been strengthened by essays from at least one or two individuals who have experienced the maelstrom as head of a large state university. Either David Hendry or Meredith Wilson could have made an important contribution.

Fred F. Harcleroad, ed.
ISSUES OF THE SEVENTIES
San Francisco: Jossey-Bass, 1970

This collection of papers was originally delivered at a conference sponsored by the American College Testing Program to commemorate its first decade of service to students and to institutions of higher education. In a sense, the title is misleading, for the collected essays do not look toward the seventies as much as back to the fifties and sixties. Nor did a number of the authors apparently stretch themselves, for what they say here is hauntingly reminiscent of what they have been saying elsewhere for a decade or more. Thus, O.

Meredith Wilson thinks national and institutional priorities have been mixed up. Nevitt Sanford believes that the real shortage in our society is a shortage of leaders. Harold Taylor thinks that campus unrest has been occasioned because students cannot attack the society directly and thus are attacking the place they know best in order to achieve what results they desire. And David P. Campbell, after first emphasizing that little is known about the impact of colleges on the students, urges diversity in our institutions, both among faculty and among students. Most of the statements are solid remarks made by experienced men, reflecting a generally accepted system of values. Perhaps the real fault is that most of the authors have written too much too recently and appeared on too many conference programs. A changing of the guard might make future compendia such as this more exciting.

Stanley Lehrer, ed.
LEADERS, TEACHERS, AND LEARNERS IN ACADEME
New York: Appleton-Century-Crofts, 1970

These articles dealing with higher education have appeared over the years in *School and Society*. Generally, the articles seem unreflective, unimaginative and cliche-ridden. Because of the nature of *School and Society*, pieces appearing there are likely to be topical and of little lasting significance. Hence, the collection of those articles is subject to the same criticism. Considerable space is devoted to the Arthur Bestor diatribes and responses about the failings of public education. In 1970 the entire Bestor controversy seems quite insignificant, overshadowed as it was by Sputnik-initiated attempts at educational reform. The papers on the college presidency are either opinions or summaries of opinions which evidence little awareness of the profound changes taking place in the whole field of academic governance. Many of the articles appear to have been prepared originally as short speeches or comments made on panel discussions, sent to *School and Society* simply as a way of getting copy out of the files. Most of the major topics necessary in an overview of higher education are represented—The University and College, The Administration, The Teacher, Professor and Scholar, The Art of Teaching, The Student—but the treatment of each reveals once again that in many respects education is really a dull subject.

John D. Margolis, ed.
THE CAMPUS IN THE MODERN WORLD
New York: Macmillan, 1970

One can only wonder why Margolis saw fit to edit this collection of twenty-five essays, selected presumably to help the reader understand the campus and higher education. The conflicts and tensions perplexing the contemporary campus are treated not at all. The vast majority of the authors favor a prescribed curriculum based largely on the Great Books tradition or its derivatives and fancy that these can be studied in the tranquility of a college campus. The editor claims at the outset that he doesn't propose to deal with contemporary conflict, hence this might excuse the exclusion of work on black studies; but there is virtually nothing in the book to indicate that education might be concerned with something other than the high intellectual tradition of Western civilization. For statements of the goals of higher education, the editor has called upon Mark Van Doren, Robert Hutchins and T. S. Eliot, and for analyses of how colleges and universities function, he uses such people as Arthur Bestor, Jacques Barzun and James A. Perkins, none of whom could be accused of being reformers. If there were need for another book of readings on higher education, including equal parts of traditional and reforming literature might better have accomplished the editor's purpose.

W. R. Niblett, ed.
HIGHER EDUCATION: DEMAND AND RESPONSE
San Francisco: Jossey-Bass, 1970

Conference Proceedings and Symposia

Seminar participants drawn from the three major English-speaking countries of the West have produced a generally thoughtful collection of papers providing historical perspective. The handling and presentation of the discussion transcripts are much better than usual. The essays will not help practice much but they do provide insight and stimulation to thought. The principal speakers for the most part value higher education deeply, see that it has run into serious problems and are questing for ways out of the wilderness. But these difficulties are now viewed in isolation, for many of them are rooted in the historic nature of the university. Nor are the problems judged as uniquely American, for parallel developments are found in Canada and in England. At the root of the many discussions is the conflict between the role of the university as a certifying agent, as a producer of knowledge, and as a helping agent in the personal development of young men and women. These essayists search for ways of accommodating all of these without disruption. There can, however, be at least one caveat to this attempt to blend historical perspective with contemporary problems. That is the tendency of some of the writers to be insufficiently aware of historical precision. Thus Edward Shoben repeats the cliche that the nineteenth century college attracted students of the well-to-do because their parents didn't know what else to do with them. Closer digest of actual letters between parents and students in the nineteenth century reveals first of all that college students did not come from the wealthy classes but the middle class intellectuals who saw college attending as an important means of upward social mobility. Hence there was no real difference between overall motivation in the first half of the nineteenth century and the second half, which saw the evolution of the land grant colleges. Then, too, a close perusal of writings of the student protesters during the 1960s doesn't really lend credence to Shoben's notion that students have resisted the social utility value of higher education. Shoben's essay seems much like the writing of one who has read one survey of Western civilization and then seeks to use profound historical truth. However, when he stays with the contemporary scene, his insights frequently are brilliant, and the same criticism could be leveled at most of the other writers in this thoroughly worthwhile book.

The Literature of Higher Education 1971

F. Robert Paulsen, ed.
CHANGING DIMENSIONS IN INTERNATIONAL EDUCATION
Tucson: University of Arizona Press, 1970

This is one of a series of conference symposia which have been put out over the past several years, none of which appears to have been particularly profound. Thus the lead essay says: "One of the reasons for [the growth of universities] has been the rapid advances in communication technology. Other means of communication have effectively reduced the size of our world and widened our horizons of concern." One really does not need to read this many more times to have the message sink in, and equally profound is the concluding note of that same essay: "A final point is that there is a need to create educational institutions that cut across national boundaries." Subsequent chapters deal with specific cases, ranging from a discussion of the Chapman College University Afloat to quite superficial descriptions of higher education in several other regions of the world. This, for the most part, is a silly, superficial book written in almost primer style. It is long on detail on some of the regional case studies but short on supportable generalization. It is long on polemical pleading for international education but quite short on historical accuracy. In a sense, this book reveals much that is wrong with the literature of higher education. It would be richer without it.

F. Robert Paulsen, ed.
HIGHER EDUCATION: DIMENSIONS AND DIRECTIONS
Tucson: University of Arizona Press, 1970

Paulsen here presents a series of lectures delivered in the College of Education at the University of Arizona during 1965–68. It is a silly book, full of cliches; none of the papers says anything new, and most repeat much that is old. The section dealing with liberal education could have opened up new ground but preferred to repeat tired shibboleths. The philosophy section had the opportunity to show caustically how philosophy had failed but could still contribute. But once again the section did not do it. The lead chapter, for example, discusses the American state university. Quoting not original evidence but Henry Steele Commager, the author establishes that times have changed. He also shows some numerical growth and indicates that universal higher education is a somewhat revolutionary idea. Proceeding on, he uses the presently rather discredited argument that economic returns to the individual are an adequate defense for higher education, then stresses the unestablished need for more and more highly trained talent which must be educated through federal support if the rapidly expanding cost of higher education is to be paid. Surely all of these things have been discussed previously and probably better. Or, dipping into another portion, it is a little bizarre that a book published in 1970 can say: "Shortages of qualified faculty members are currently a besetting problem for colleges and universities." It is the sort of hyperbole contained in most of these essays which so clutters up the literature of higher education and makes the task of finding a worthwhile book to receive an award an especially frustrating experience.

G. Kerry Smith, ed.
THE TROUBLED CAMPUS: CURRENT ISSUES IN HIGHER EDUCATION
San Francisco: Jossey-Bass, 1970

In selected papers delivered at the March 1970 National Conference on Higher Education, the book seeks to elaborate a discussion of the troubled society, how that society is reflected on campus, and the options which are available to higher education in coping with times of trouble. The authors of the papers are for the most part reasonably well known and have been speaking their minds for some time. Thus Buell Gallagher, Harlan Cleveland, Morris Keaton, Max Wise, and Lyman Glenny all have contributed essays.

The Literature of Higher Education 1971

Perhaps because of the tensions which were being experienced by higher education in 1969, the essays seem to possess a greater amount of passion, hence intrinsic interest, than has been true of proceedings from that conference in years past.

UNIVERSITY DEVELOPMENT, CONTINUITY AND CHANGE
Beirut: American University of Beirut, 1969

The papers from a Colloquium on Higher Education for Administrators in Middle East Institutions are presented. Earl J. McGrath makes a series of presentations with amplifying papers presented by educators from the Middle East. Generally, McGrath's position, which is refined in a series of statements, is that the governance of higher education must be restructured to allow faculty, students and other elements a greater voice. Yet at the same time he believes central administration should reassert prerogatives essential to stable governance. Although McGrath does not say so, he appears to believe in what Keaton and Hodgkinson have called elsewhere "the non-zero sub game." That is, McGrath appears to want to have it both ways—faculty, students, alumni, all gaining power while administration also gains power. As do some of the other contributors, McGrath feels that higher education is a genuine field of study and that there is a body of useful generalization. A number of the papers suggest that education is a rational activity and that techniques for such things as the teaching of values can be developed. In general, the contributions seem fresher than most one finds in conference literature, and although a number of the amplifying papers deal with a Middle Eastern or European context, they all seem relevant to the American experience. The book probably will not be given the wide circulation it deserves.

Nine

✫✫✫✫✫✫✫✫✫✫✫✫✫✫✫

TEACHING AND OTHER PROFESSIONAL PROCEDURES

✫✫✫✫✫✫✫✫✫✫✫✫✫✫✫

It has always appeared strange that the central acts in the practice of education are so poorly and sparsely described in the literature. It is as though in medicine the acts of history-taking, use of diagnostic tools and surgical procedures were left to chance, while textbooks stressed the philosophy of medicine. This year's supply is not bad but it is still slight.

Kenneth E. Eble
THE RECOGNITION AND EVALUATION
OF TEACHING
Salt Lake City: Project to Improve College Teaching, 1970

Commissioned by The Project to Improve College Teaching (jointly sponsored by A.A.U.P. and A.A.C.) Eble has prepared a not unreadable book on attempts to evaluate college teaching. He implicitly argues that student evaluation of teaching is reasonably effective and ought to be practiced more widely. In analyzing why student evaluation is not more prevalent, the author mentions faculty anxieties, unhealthy competition among faculty members, a tendency for evaluation forms to push teaching into ever more formalized and mechanical molds, and student inability to maintain a consistently reliable evaluative posture. But he also indicates that when he actually began to explore attitudes toward evaluation of teaching, he found much less faculty resistance than he had anticipated. For those familiar with McKeachie's writings on college teaching, the book will not hold much that is new; but it is just possible that a few of the stronger statements will find their way into campus reports and that programs to evaluate teaching will eventually become more widespread.

Laurene E. Fitzgerald, Walter F. Johnson, Willa Norris
COLLEGE STUDENT PERSONNEL
Boston: Houghton Mifflin, 1970

This peculiar collection of papers, written for the most part by leaders in the student personnel movement over the past twenty-five years, purports to present the state of the art and the state of the movement. The authors believe that student personnel work is still

Teaching and Other Professional Procedures

very much in process of emerging as a profession and is struggling to gain an identity and to delineate its function. The essays in aggregate clearly reveal the struggle but the prognosis of the subprofession stands somewhat in doubt. There seems general agreement that student personnel work should try to humanize higher education, to individualize it, to establish some balance in the world of the student, to nurture and extend a student's drives, interests and motives so that he can use the total college community for educational purposes, and to enhance immediate satisfactions and enjoyments students derive from their college experience. These apparently have governed much of the effort in the past and seem to be accepted as guidelines for emergence of the subprofession in the future. In the years ahead, student personnel people wish to establish the preeminence of the quality of human relationships, decentralize services and locate them where students are. They want also to eliminate the tendency to view students as only falling in the age range 18 to 21, and to give attention to more mature people, to contribute to students' non-work life, and to help students examine value differences in a changing culture. Sensitive to changing times, future student personnel work should give more attention to the problems of women, the transfer student, and the creatively different. The personnel worker should probably encourage philosophy and religion as elements in student lives and should seek to develop highly personalized and confidential relationships with students. All of this is well and good, but the book still must be viewed as somewhat anachronistic. The section dealing with the doctrine of *in loco parentis* presents several points of view; but one can wonder about the inclusion in something other than an antiquarian history of an essay which ends:

> *The writer cannot help but feel that any departure from the legal principle of* in loco parentis *will work a hardship upon a number of students who may transgress but not rebel, as it will take away a protection that is now built in to the system. Disciplinary action will become a punitive action and not an educational experience.*

One also wonders about a 1970 book dealing with student personnel workers which does not contain long sections on handling student protest and violence. Actually, only one essay focuses on contemporary problems, and that one does so but lightly. As a historical document the book has value, but as an important source material for student personnel workers in training, one can have serious doubts as to its value.

Guy R. Lyle
THE LIBRARIAN SPEAKING
Athens: University of Georgia Press, 1970

The book was relegated to the bottom of the pile of those to be reviewed in 1970 because the title somehow implied a high degree of preciousness. But on examination the volume turns out to be a collection of quite well-edited interviews with distinguished American university librarians, during which they comment clearly and without jargon on a number of professional and technical problems facing their profession. Each chapter is devoted to one librarian and is organized around a series of well-contrived questions and the responses of the interviewee. Here one can obtain informed judgment about the values of storage libraries for large universities, whether university libraries can even attempt to remain faithful to the ideal once expressed—that university libraries should try to acquire everything. Also included are strategies and techniques for increasing the professional stature of professional librarians. For professional librarians this book should be great fun, for the editing conveys the impression of skillful and informed conversation about matters of daily concern. Even for students of higher education the view of the university from the steps of the library is a different one and one worth considering.

Melvene D. Hardee
FACULTY ADVISING IN COLLEGES AND UNIVERSITIES
Washington: American College Personnel Association, 1970

Teaching and Other Professional Procedures

The author argues that faculty members, although trained in disciplines, can be motivated and prepared to offer a much broader brand of advisement to students than that implied by faculty preparation. The entire treatment, although admirably documented with what is really going on, seems primarily an updating of a system of faculty advising which long has prevailed at Stephens College. There, every faculty member and academic administrator is expected to advise a number of students. Hardee has long favored that approach and appears still to do so. She summarizes a wealth of information about advising, testifying that the use of advisers is plausible. However, she does not really address the central question: how to persuade faculty members, especially in large research-oriented institutions, to become members of a helping profession. There can be some doubt that this miracle can be brought to pass. But perhaps the book is not really intended for the large research-oriented university. If the approach is studied carefully by faculties in junior colleges, liberal arts colleges and some of the state colleges, it will have affected ultimately quite a large proportion of college students. More can scarcely be expected from any book. Thus the American College Personnel Association should be commended for sponsoring this Number 9 in its Series on Student Personnel.

Win Kelly, Leslie Wilbur
TEACHING IN THE AMERICAN JUNIOR COLLEGE
New York: Appleton-Century-Crofts, 1970

For those preparing for junior college teaching this text has considerable value. It reviews the history of the junior college movement and establishes that while the broad origins are clear, the specific events are not. It tries to define growth stages of the junior college, from the earliest attempts to provide relief for universities from lower division instruction to the present preoccupation with a comprehensive program. The authors for the most part agree with dogma of the present Establishment in the junior college movement and accept almost without question that a college can provide general education, transfer education, vocational education, adult education, counseling, and at the same time be a focus of community service. Their descriptions of the professional concomitants of teaching in junior colleges seem to be true and revealing. Thus they summarize average faculty salaries, fringe benefits and the like, and establish that teaching in a junior college is increasingly a comfortable professional role. They communicate quite clearly that the mission of the junior college calls for a much more teaching-oriented individual than does the university or four-year college. They present a reasonable encyclopedia of the major techniques of teaching, ranging from lectures to the Socratic method, formal discussions, debate, student reports, honor seminars, team approaches, and the technological methods. However, these are not treated in sufficient detail to allow a novice teacher the nerve necessary to experiment with new approaches. They present an adequate but not exhaustive bibliography and, since it is a textbook, suggest some questions for student discussion and consideration. Generally, those questions focus on specific problems rather than broad philosophic or theoretical problems, and this is probably right. There apparently is a growing market for such a text; this can be commended for beginning classes but for none other.

William H. Morris, ed.
EFFECTIVE COLLEGE TEACHING
Washington, D.C.: American Council on Education, 1970

This consists of a number of commissioned papers dealing with problems, perplexities and issues in college teaching. The book is intended to help particularly younger teachers and teaching assistants, and it strives to make teaching respectable by offering commentary by educationists and by distinguished representatives of some of the learned professions. Thus the book first discusses general theories about teaching and some general techniques such as grading, examinations, and the like, applicable to most fields. Then it considers the problems of teaching mathematics, science, social science and the humanities—and these sections offer considerable richness in tips on actual teaching performance. Lastly, the volume presents to the young teacher a description of the bureaucratic conditions within which college teaching is conducted. The book generally seems less pedestrian than most attempts to discuss teaching as an applied art. But still one comes away without any sense of wonder or mystery. It could just be that teaching is really as dull as descriptions of it sound; but if this is true, why the continued appeal of the role? The book in total represents one major achievement; that is, it culminated from a series of working sessions held by professional educators and representatives of the learned societies. If that sort of conversation could be continued, the rewards might be great.

Stephen J. Miller
PRESCRIPTION FOR LEADERSHIP
Chicago: Aldine, 1970

The author, having used participant-observer techniques, tries to show how highly selected young doctors are enculturated into a medical élite by serving residencies in the Harvard Medical Unit of Boston City Hospital. Graduates from this residency program have consistently made their way into important positions of leadership in American medicine and particularly in American academic medicine. Graduates are generally recognized within the profession as being outstandingly capable and the profession seems willing to accord this group the status of an élite. This group, partly through power to perpetuate itself, has been able to maintain its position. Individuals accepted for residencies come from all sorts of medical schools; the largest number come from Harvard but the lesser known, or lesser recognized, institutions are by no means excluded. Thus the Medical Unit is selective but not necessarily along an institutional dimension. Once the intern starts to work he is subject not only to the formal educational processes but to a vast array of informal influences; and he must learn how to respond to those. The author appears to have been an accurate observer and the quotes from interviews suggest he was able to relate well enough to interns so that they talked about what bothered them. However, his attempt to fit all of these observations into some theoretical mold does not quite come off. The final chapter concludes that much of formal education for a professional is somewhat irrelevant to what the professional will be doing; but that the internship or field experience, properly organized through both formal and informal influences, is a major formative device. Increasingly, other professions are seeing the values of an internship, and this last chapter might be informative to them. The intern receives as much value from developing the self-concept of a professional as from acquiring actual clinical competencies. Both are important.

Anthony G. Oetinger
RUN, COMPUTER, RUN
Cambridge, Mass.: Harvard University Press, 1969

The author clearly believes in the ultimate educational potential of newer media and new technology, but he recognizes that visionary portrayals of what is possible are highly overdrawn and far from presently realizable. On the one hand, there is the dream of multi-media education including computer-assisted instruction, quickly accessible video tapes and automated access to the great libraries of the world available in any classroom in the country. This vision will fall short because ultimately the information available at terminals must be prepared by people, and the available people will probably not have enough ideas or enough command of the technology to interest students for a sustained period of time. Education's failure to use existing technology to achieve the goal for which it is best designed—efficiency—has stemmed primarily from a failure to follow essential maxims. If efficiency is desired, promising ideas must be supported longer than they are now. Risk-taking must be supported and failure cushioned. Risks, resources, and responsibilities must be shared by all partners in the educational enterprise. Efficiency requires human judgment, not decision by formula. To gain efficiency, support in depth must be provided for a number of diverse alternatives. Ultimately, of course, the technology will be used, but not until much more realistic thinking is applied. After having read so much of the Utopian literature, this book is indeed refreshing.

James M. Salem
THE TEACHER AS A WRITER: PAUL T. NOLAN EXAMPLE
Metuchen, N.J.: Scarecrow Press, 1970

The underlying thesis of this odd book is that for some people there should be a direct and visible relationship between the act of teaching and the act of writing. It argues that well-prepared lectures, critiques or discussions can be then reconstituted and published. The object of the study apparently viewed himself consistently as a full-time teacher who also got a great deal of satisfaction from publishing; and he apparently did what many of us do, which is to rework lecture notes and the like into articles, collections of essays, textbooks and monographs. The bulk of the book consists of examples of published materials which could be used in college classes dealing with literature. They are generally well-written, erudite, and if read as occasional pieces seem worthy of book-length publication, but they are more idiosyncratic than effectively didactic, for the book offers little but exhortation in helping other teachers decide whether or not to combine teaching and publication.

Ten

CURRICULUM

The judgment made about teaching could also be made about the curriculum. There just is not a consistent bibliography about the curriculum. It is good, however, that the arts and humanities are finally getting some attention—especially in such thoughtful works as Levi's *The Humanities Today*.

>James Steve Counelis, ed.
>TO BE A PHOENIX
>Bloomington, Ind.: Phi Delta Kappa, 1969

This collection of essays, apparently prepared specifically for the volume, attempts to delineate the role of the professor of education, to anticipate directions of role emergence, and possibly to imply guidelines for the education of professors. That the education professoriate is a perplexity should be in no doubt, nor does this book leave any. It was traditionally composed of people with considerable practical experience in education who tried to teach other practitioners and slowly became a stepchild of the rest of the university community, trying to assume academic pretensions while keeping the practitioner flavor. The present struggle is to develop multidisciplinary competence to examine the problems of education. The profession gained considerable stature shortly after the turn of the century when men such as Cubberley, Thorndike, Judd, and Dewey made an enormous impact on the practice of education. There followed a long hiatus in which the professoriate produced no intellectual innovations, and generally exploited the earlier seminal ideas. A more recent movement seeks to attract more people from other disciplines who can focus on the problems of education as anthropologists, sociologists, or philosophers. As this quest for academic rigor and respectability proceeds, there is clear implication that the concerns of practitioners will be treated at a much more theoretical level. Whether or not this is in the public interest, of course, may be questioned. The implications for training are clearly explicit in this book. More work outside professional education and more rigorous training in related disciplines are desirable. The prose in this small volume does not ring, nor does the presumed logic of the presentation emerge.

Albert William Levi
THE HUMANITIES TODAY
Bloomington: Indiana University Press, 1970

Levi has made a valiant, although not completely successful try to clarify thinking about the humanities. He believes that if the humanities are to play an important role in education and in life, they must be recognized as essentially different from other forms of knowledge. And he attempts to point up this distinctiveness through a logical equation. He argues that the humanities are not the natural sciences, social sciences, nor fine arts; that the humanities are identical with the liberal arts, which consist of the arts of communication, continuity and criticism. So far, so good. But when he attempts to show the contribution to human development which these liberal arts or humanities can make, he encounters but never accommodates problems of pedantry, aridity, and overemphasis on behaviorism, even within the humanities. The author is somewhat suspicious of claims, such as those made by William Arrowsmith, that the humanists themselves have betrayed the humanities, or the claims made by supporters of a foundation for the humanities that the humanities teach values and judgment, that they reveal wisdom and ethics and enable people to ask and to answer what it means to live well. Then, in his concluding chapter, he seems to be saying essentially the same thing:

> *The humanities can not be dismissed. Far from being outmoded, they are the eternally relevant, precisely because they are the arts of communication, the arts of continuity and the arts of criticism. Language remains the indispensable medium within which we move and breathe. History provides that group memory which makes the communal bond possible. Philosophic criticism is the only activity through which man's self reflection modifies the conditions of his existence. The cup of the humanities, however, must be the vessel from which we drink our life.*

An additional question can be raised. While the elimination of the fine and performing arts can be understood on logical grounds, one wonders if leaving those arts out of the purview of the humanities is really defensible. There could be justification for arguing that many of the values Levi claims for the liberal arts could be best provided contemporary college students through the fine and performing arts, even through studio experience. Nonetheless, this slim collection of essays ought to find itself on the shelves of faculty reading rooms and should be examined in detail by any faculty attempting a curricular revision.

Curriculum

Jerome P. Lysaught
AN ABSTRACT FOR ACTION
New York: McGraw-Hill, 1970

This reports on a commission-style study of nursing education and follows a number of other significant studies which have been made to bring nursing into the professional mainstream. It probes the various issues: whether hospital training of nurses or nursing education within the university context is better, dysfunctions in careers of nurses, the problems of supply and demand, the preparation and continuing upgrading of nursing faculties, and the phenomenon of increased production but underutilization of nurses. Generally, the commission came out in favor of lodging nursing education clearly within the university. If some hospitals were to continue their programs, close affiliation should be made with nearby universities. The commission believes that improvement of nursing education is at least a statewide problem and hence urges statewide planning within a framework established by a national commission on medicine and nursing. The essential problem, however, is really not educational but social. In 1948 a study of nursing stated, "Only when abiding conviction of social worth replaces lack of self-confidence, negativism and carping comment will that climate of opinion be created whereby nursing can look forward to greater selectivity of personnel and to a level of nursing care that bespeak growth and development for the nurse herself and more and better health service for society." This 1970 study reaffirms that this still is the essential issue.

Lewis B. Mayhew
GRADUATE AND PROFESSIONAL EDUCATION 1980
New York: McGraw-Hill, 1970

Basing his findings on two different studies, the author observes that if present plans are realized, the United States will be producing on the order of seventy thousand PhDs by 1980. A large number of institutions, which he calls "developing institutions," are making plans for rapid entry into master's level work and subsequently doctoral level work in emulation of the thirty or forty prestige universities currently producing the largest number of doctorates. These aspirations are tenaciously held even though nothing in an institution's history suggests that it has the potentiality to offer first-rate graduate work. Plans as expressed do not appear particularly innovative; the pacesetting institutions will simply do better what they are now doing, and the developing institutions will seek to do what the pacesetters have done. One surprise is that humanistic fields appear headed for much more rapid growth than the scientific fields. Quite clearly, institutions have been led into this interest in graduate work by a number of forces. One of the most significant is federal policy. In spite of presidential disclaimers to the contrary, institutions do see entry into graduate work as being economically sound, and professors, of course, see graduate work as a fitting culmination for their own professional careers. Whether the plans as expressed will materialize cannot be known. Perhaps if the lack of placement of recent recipients of PhDs continues, institutions may back away from the precipitous rush into graduate work.

Margaret Mahoney
THE ARTS ON CAMPUS
Greenwich, Conn.: New York Graphic Society, 1970

A collection of essays written to establish the need for change in art education suggests ways to restructure educational goals and course work and outlines broad categories of reform. The overall point of view of the book is summed up in a concluding statement:

> *There is no conflict between studying the arts as fields of inquiry and learning about the arts in the context of the broader objective. It is up to the colleges to reconcile the differences that cause the apparent conflict: the differences between discipline, between scholar and artist, and between styles. Recon-*

Curriculum

ciliation can come about only if colleges will make (in John Roush's words) opportunity full and learning efficient for students of all shades of talent and intellectual capability. Many faculty members and administrators would claim that this is the purpose of the undergraduate education as it is now carried out.

Joel C. Mickelson, ed.
AMERICAN PERSONALITY AND THE CREATIVE ARTS
Minneapolis: Burgess, 1969

At first blush this volume seems rather unrelated to higher education. However, the title is a misnomer, for the book explicates the evolution of an important area of interdisciplinary work. It seeks to show how the field of American studies emerged because traditional literary criticism, history and rudimentary theology did not provide the needed synthesis. The effort to fashion a new field, using techniques which are considered currently quite new, is bringing together professors and some graduate students from several fields to discuss some problem of American culture which might be viewed as an interdisciplinary phenomenon. Some of these early seminars disrupted over the age-long controversy as to whether works of art are essences in themselves or should be viewed as simply cultural documents. Gradually, it would appear that the culturists have gained sway, and contemporary efforts in American studies use the concept of culture taken from anthropologists as one of the crystallizing agents. A number of the essays which consider discrete phenomena in America, such as American women, or American art, reflect a high order of trans-disciplinary scholarship, showing what things are possible if sufficient talent and resources are brought to bear. But this book is more than an historical resumé. Some of the ideas would seem to have relevance for the emerging disciplinary field of black studies; and it is just possible that persons interested in the field of higher education as an object of study could also profit from examining the methods and pitfalls experienced by those who helped create the field of American studies. Several of the essays seem just a bit precious, but perhaps this is to be expected in view of the disciplines contributing to this new interdisciplinary field.

James W. Reynolds
THE COMPREHENSIVE JUNIOR COLLEGE CURRICULUM
Berkeley: McCutchan, 1970

This book was intended as one of a series on college administration published by McCutchan—a series which was discontinued after only a few books. The author's point of view rests on a conception of community colleges which offer general education, transfer curricula, technical and vocational curricula, adult education, and which also serve as a focus for community service. Within each of those fields Reynolds describes quite accurately what courses are offered and at least some of the problems in offering them. Junior or community colleges probably have not thought through any theoretical formulation of their curricula; thus all the material that is available has to be reportorial. Toward the end of the book Reynolds does deal with some theoretical issues, such as articulation and possible limits to curricular offerings. However, treating these separate matters does not result in an all-encompassing theory. The book is an excellent first step in producing a needed literature on the curriculum. It should enrich considerably the education of people entering junior college teaching and administration. One hopes that after several years the book will be redone with a less eclectic and more consistent overall theory or philosophy of curriculum. In response to the problems and perplexities of the 1960s, institutions, individuals and conferences are all addressing themselves to the problems of academic governance. Out of this ferment will eventually come some synthesis, but at present there is a host of conflicting points of view.

Curriculum

Neil J. Smelser, James A. Davis, eds.
SOCIOLOGY
Englewood Cliffs, N.J.: Prentice-Hall, 1969

As one of the commissioned sub-studies of the survey of the behavioral and social sciences conducted by The National Academy of Sciences, this book is intended to introduce the general reader to the present state of sociology by presenting vignettes of classical and contemporary sociological research. It attempts to portray a discipline steadily moving toward maturity and respectability. The descriptive materials are not bad but the recommendations seem painfully banal, calling for diversified undergraduate curricula, empirical research experience for undergraduates, improved undergraduate teaching, and expansion of graduate programs and research. Higher standards of graduate admissions are advanced in the light of recent serious questioning of techniques used to screen and admit graduate students. At least, however, there is a utilitarian vein running throughout the report which does suggest that sociological research ought to contribute to solving human problems.

Eleven

✫✫✫✫✫✫✫✫✫✫✫✫✫✫✫

ECONOMIC ANALYSES OF BASIC ASSUMPTIONS

✫✫✫✫✫✫✫✫✫✫✫✫✫✫✫

For years economists paid little or no attention to higher education as an economic institution. Fortunately, this attitude is changing, and at least a few of these examples should produce serious questioning of assumptions.

Economic Analyses of Basic Assumptions

Ivar Berg
EDUCATION AND JOBS: THE GREAT
TRAINING ROBBERY
New York: Praeger, 1970

This significant book is a systematic examination of the American mythology that education is necessary for successful job performance. Behind much of the expansion of education, especially higher education, has been the belief that increased formal training was necessary for successful performance of jobs in an increasingly technological society. Through a series of field studies, tenure of workers, judgment of worker performance, and educational and intelligence levels were examined. What the author generally finds is that the relationship between educational level and job performance is most frequently nonexistent or negative. The author does not believe necessarily that educational requirements are bad, but educational requirements do not produce the sorts of results managers believe they do. "To argue that well educated people will boost efficiency, improve organizations, and so on, may be to misunderstand in a fundamental way the nature of American education which functions to an important, indeed depressing extent as a licensing agency." The major implication from this study is that American education should be redirected so that more people finish the twelfth grade and achieve basic comprehension of reading and number skills, rather than unevenly extending education for others to higher levels of training on the faulty assumption that the more training, the more effective the worker. In effect, the author argues that there is no good reason for education to persist in the credentialing business. Business and industry are apparently quite capable of providing credentials based on actual job performance.

Gunnar Boalt, Herman Lantz
UNIVERSITIES AND RESEARCH
New York: Wiley, 1970

The Literature of Higher Education 1971

In a somewhat pretentious way, the authors utilize sociological theory and techniques to examine the part research and writing play in the contemporary university. They first note that the rise of research emphases in universities has placed many academic men in serious role conflict situations, finding that teaching does not carry with it rewards, and that research, in one way or another, is frequently unfeasible. For some, the way out of the dilemma is to accept an administrative role which carries with it some of the perquisites that go to research professors. However, a career in administration may mean adopting a managerial ideology, whereas professors have been socialized into being quite suspicious of management and its correlates of efficiency, order, regulations and control. After presenting these not particularly secret factors, the authors turn first to a hypothetical study and then provide details of an actual study showing relationships between individual values and actual professional activities. Using collections of PhD and master's theses, they attempted to classify the various values represented. Then in a series of quite disjointed chapters the authors tried to describe how they manipulated their information to throw light on the problem they were studying. The final chapter presents a series of conclusions which, on examination, turn out to be either generally accepted truisms or scarcely intelligible statements. For example, they say, not unsurprisingly, universities are given more prestige the larger they are and the greater budget they have. Or, the equally profound statement: "The academic tries to take the role best suited to his interests and capacity and tries to maximize his benefits." But too much of this section is this sort:

> *If our sample includes scientific writings of all kinds, there would be a number of ambitious dissertations taking good care of many scientific values, and also a number of very bad articles with low grades. This would tend to give positive correlations between the grades of all values, just one cluster containing all values. We call that pattern the unified value pattern. If, however, our sample was chosen so that all the*

Economic Analyses of Basic Assumptions

publications had had about the same research resources, they would vary rather little in scientific effort but instead in the direction of this effort. Then we expect a matrix with clear-cut clusters, the values correlated positively with values in the same cluster, and negatively with values in competing clusters. If our sample is somewhat in the middle between these two extremes, the two tendencies (positive correlations between classes of publications, negative correlations within classes) would neutralize each other and give a matrix with some clusters of positively correlated variables but very low correlations between variables of different clusters. We call this the compromise pattern.

It is such foolishness, traveling under the guise of scientific inquiry, which tends to make intellectuals generally suspect.

Robert H. Connery, ed.
THE CORPORATION AND THE CAMPUS
New York: Praeger, 1970

Presented here is a collection of papers delivered at a conference jointly sponsored by The Academy of Political Science and the Council for Financial Aid to Education. Spokesmen from higher education analyzed a number of different issues, while spokesmen from the corporate world either responded or indicated areas of possible cooperation between education and the business community. The overall impression is that the spokesmen for business were responsible, far-seeing and willing to accept the necessity for substantially increased corporate support for higher education during the seventies. There was little carping about campus unrest, although one might have expected some of this to creep in. There was little complaint that institutions might have been somewhat inefficient in their past management of affairs and funds. Nor was there much of the "bull" mentality implying that higher education during the seventies should be much less expansionist. Indeed, the positive things stated should make those concerned with the management of higher education exceedingly hopeful for the future. Major business units and leading universities are expected to assume responsibility for remedying some of society's critical social and environmental ills. Although other segments will be asking the business community for assistance, the corporate world should try hard to maintain increased rates of giving to higher education, perhaps even at the rate of a ten per cent increase per year for the decade. There was general recognition that enlightened leadership is essential if corporations are going to act responsibly, and there was evidence that each year more and more top business leadership is willing to provide assistance for higher education. While the papers delivered by the academicians seemed adequate, they typically did not reflect as much willingness to change, to grow and to examine previously held assumptions. Indeed, the voices from the university sounded quite orthodox. Thus, universities employing their customary instrumentalities were urged to simply redirect the focus of attention and try to solve such vexing questions as the urban condition. After reviewing the research record of American universities since World War II, the academics requested continued support—despite strong suspicions of some that, outside of major breakthroughs in the health sciences and physical sciences, university research as presently conducted was quite ineffective and unproductive during those two decades. It was recognized that institutions ought properly to concern themselves with such things as black studies and changed admissions patterns for disadvantaged youth; but there seemed no predisposition to examine radical new ways of dealing with those matters. Particularly with respect to management and governance did representatives from the university seem self-satisfied. The argument was advanced that universities as peculiar entities could not be expected to operate efficiently as determined by short-run measures. Rather, there was almost the implication that serendipity was to be expected and used as the criterion for university success. Several spokesmen did examine the possibilities of some financial and management palliatives, but no one suggested the fundamental deployment of resources characteristic of universities might be seriously reexamined. The book is a substantial contribution to the

Economic Analyses of Basic Assumptions

literature of higher education for it does bring together under one cover much of an emerging conventional wisdom about institutions and the corporate world. And the book does hang together much better than most conference proceedings. Since it is not overly long, it might well be used as a working paper for board of trustee seminars, which the boards of at least major universities might consider holding. Because a reasonably high number of trustees come from the corporate world, such seminars might help insure the wider reading which *The Corporation and the Campus* deserves but will probably not receive.

John K. Folger, Helen S. Astin, Alan E. Bayer
HUMAN RESOURCES AND HIGHER EDUCATION
New York: Russell Foundation, 1970

The need for such a book as this is urgent. During the several decades just past, American educational society has fluctuated wildly in anticipating and producing needed professional and technical manpower. A potential oversupply of PhD recipients illustrates past failures in predicting demand and shifts within and without colleges and universities. Now John Folger and his associates have compiled what should be a major contribution to educational planners. They analyze the weakness of previous manpower studies, point out methodological improvements which make manpower inquiry a more precise activity, and summarize and interpret cautiously present information about the needs of professional and technical fields and the flow of people into and through the educational system. Generally, the authors take the stand that while in a few professional fields supply is in full progress toward meeting demand, the overall public requirements for professionally and technically trained people are likely to be such that supply of college-trained individuals will not be excessive in the foreseeable future. The authors also seemingly accept the conventional wisdom that more and more education is good for more and more people and that those individuals possessing the potential for advanced training who drop out of the system represent a serious waste of human resources. Based on those two premises, the major purpose of this book may be inferred as being to contrive ways to open the educational system both for reasons of social utility and individual fulfillment.

A summary of such a comprehensive analysis is virtually impossible. The authors anticipate continued expansion of enrollments in higher education but with a continued problem of guiding young people into high-demand careers. Although there is a general softening of demand for advanced degree holders in the arts and sciences, saturation in all fields is still some distance off. The generations-old expectation of a steady 50 per cent attrition during the college years seems to be breaking down, and particularly those students who enroll initially in four-year institutions tend ultimately to graduate in much higher proportions. Since women increasingly spend time in the trained labor market, the failure of colleges and universities to prepare adequate numbers appropriately is becoming painfully apparent. However, what the content of future training programs should be for them or for other college graduates is even more unknown currently than was previously supposed. The relationship between predictors of academic aptitude, success in college courses and subsequent vocational success long supposed to be a positive one has recently come under serious scrutiny. Theorists can no longer be sanguine that a given educational program will produce effectively trained workers or sanguine about the relationship of increased educational ability of a population to economic health and productivity. The overall impact of the book deservedly should be great. However, the authors may be taken to task on several grounds. They refer a number of times to the increasing contribution to manpower studies of economists and yet do not elaborate some of the skepticism which recent economic analyses have produced regarding the benefits from higher education and the question of who should pay for it. Seemingly the authors have accepted the item of public policy calling for low- or no-cost higher education, without examining at least theoretically whether this dictum is regressive or not. This criticism should be qualified by stating that the authors' position can be arrived at only through inference, for at no time do they make such a flat assertion. Then, too, the authors seem to anticipate almost universal exposure to post-secondary education. However, they do not seem to give much attention to the possibility that given the present expressions of post-secondary education, enrolling beyond 65 or 70 per cent of a high school graduating class in any meaningful program in existing junior colleges, area vocational schools or four-year institutions may be an exercise in futility. They do not examine the possibility that increasing enrollments toward the universal level while at the same time increasing quite premature dropout rates might not be the best social policy. That is, the authors seem not to take seriously what may be a growing attitude within American society that all youth would not really profit by attendance at a post-secondary formal educational institution. Raising this question should not imply that the authors should have taken a different position. But it does suggest that comprehensive views of manpower and higher education should at least examine forcefully advanced counterviews to the conventional wisdom.

W. Lee Hansen, Burton E. Weisbrod
BENEFITS, COST AND FINANCE OF PUBLIC HIGHER EDUCATION
Chicago: Markham, 1969

This is a tightly reasoned attempt to arrive at a policy decision on the question of who shall pay for higher education, by using the tools of economic analysis. While the authors in the end admit that they have not been able to reach a set of policy recommendations, the questions their analyses raise should help responsible groups move toward policy formulations. Thus, they analyze costs of public higher education to the parent and to the state and reach the interesting conclusion that the state's actual contribution to the education of individuals may not be recouped ultimately in the form of increased taxes, as was formerly supposed. In California, the state's contribution to an individual obtaining a bachelor's degree the cheapest way possible, two years in a junior college and two years in a state college, is just about the same as the anticipated increase in tax yield permitted by the increased earning capacity which the baccalaureate degree is presumed to provide. When one adds the additional costs of state services for a growing population attracted in part by the availability of low-cost public education, the expense to a state becomes significantly greater than the contribution individuals would actually make over their lifetime. Thus a derivative of this argument is the hypothesis that perhaps California in the long run might have profited more through refraining from the creation of an elaborate low-cost system of higher education. By using the full cost of education as a basic figure, the authors find that proportionately even doubling tuition in state-supported higher education would not be enough. The authors nowhere extrapolate and come out in support of increased tuition, but this book clearly, by implication, allows for increases in tuition as a realistic solution to financing problems. The perplexities of the authors are suggested in a concluding statement which says:

> *Our own assessment is that although we have been able to point out the relevance of a number of concepts, e.g., marginal cost pricing, value added pricing, external benefits (to persons other than students) we have been unable to show how these concepts can be made operational. Our frustration in this respect is matched, however, by the firmness of our view that educational finance decisions can not be made on a more rational basis until economists and other social scientists and educators turn their attention to quantifying these cost and benefit concepts.*

Laurie M. Sharp
EDUCATION AND EMPLOYMENT
Baltimore: Johns Hopkins Press, 1970

Economic Analyses of Basic Assumptions

The book summarizes findings and interpretations derived from a set of studies conducted from 1959 to 1969 under the sponsorship of the National Science Foundation through its Manpower Study Group. For the most part, the results do not seem particularly surprising. However, one factor stands out as being at variance with much which has previously been believed. This is that the undergraduate major is probably the most important factor in a student's subsequent career. There is strong evidence, says the author, that even for liberal arts students the final choice of a college major represents a strong vocational commitment. However, this generalization might be challenged on the ground that the broad curricular and vocational categories were simply so gross as to conceal some very real differences between undergraduate preparation and what one subsequently does. This is not to say that the generalization may not be warranted, but the book is unpersuasive on the point. Moving on, the study does show that subsequent completion of graduate work is more likely when the advanced work is built on undergraduate. It is also reasonable to accept the notion that better academically prepared students go on to graduate work much more frequently than do the less academically prepared. To this reviewer it is not surprising, although to some it may be, that contrary to the "While you're up, get me a grant" milieu, most graduate students do not receive institutional financial support. (Clearly, however, there are some differences among fields.) Women, although they out-achieve male students in undergraduate schools, are substantially underrepresented in graduate and professional work. A finding clearly consistent with much revisionist research is that the reputation of the institution attended is not particularly related to subsequent vocational success. "Students who graduated from middle-level institutions, where much of the growth in the enrollment has taken place in recent years, exhibited impressive post-college career and study patterns." It is the undergraduate major rather than the institution attended which has the greatest impact on career outcomes. The book in no way negates the quest for liberalizing values in the undergraduate college but does stress the sometimes forgotten value that college attendance has an important vocational component. Ann Scott, a historian at Duke University, from examining letters of eighteenth century and nineteenth century collegians found that the same thing held true then. Hence, this book should really come as no big surprise.

Kenneth Underwood
THE CHURCH, THE UNIVERSITY, AND SOCIAL POLICY
Middletown, Conn.: Wesleyan University Press, 1969

One of the most difficult of recent books to assess is this report of an elaborate study of the campus ministry, which was supported by the Danforth Foundation and cost more than a third of a million dollars. It seeks to delineate a role, based on evidence and theological considerations, for the campus minister whereby he may bring about radical reformation of the entire Protestant Church. The author is struggling toward a conception of an entirely new brand of scholarship which he calls policy research. He uses evidence, information, insight from many different fields and disciplines in an action-oriented process which ultimately can not only produce policy statements but bring about policy change as well. The study proceeded by first commissioning a number of substudies to obtain empirical evidence about such things as how campus ministers perceived themselves, what their roles actually were in their universities, and what were perceived problems within the corporate church. These data, together with theologically based position papers and the observations and insights of participants themselves, were analyzed, discussed, pondered, and reported on by a number of policy research centers scattered throughout the United States. As the results of these deliberations poured into the central office of the study, the project director pondered them in the light of his own theoretical and theological orientation and fashioned a new statement. In language somewhat difficult to comprehend, the author seeks to establish the mission of the campus minister in a theological context and then extrapolates the ways in which the campus minister does and could

Economic Analyses of Basic Assumptions

function. Had the author stopped at this point, there could be no serious quarrel. However, he seems to be making the claim, but with no other support than his own assertion, that the campus ministry is becoming the truly vitalizing force in Protestant Christianity. What he is struggling for in the social policy portion of his argument are ways to make this emergent role effective; and here his perceptions simply do not square with my own. It is true that some stimulating literature is coming out of departments of theology and campus chaplaincies, particularly on some of the great secular university campuses. However, one does not have the impression that these are affecting either large populations of students or faculties on those campuses; nor are they taken too seriously by the laymen in Protestant congregations. As for the future, Underwood wants to maintain a series of policy centers to work continuously at revitalizing the corporate church and the Christian mission, and this is a worthy goal if such activities can be supported. This long and burdensome work could well become a significant document in theological circles, and possibly of considerable significance for seminary education. It would need to be shortened and restyled in a less specialized idiom if it were to have major impact on the odd processes of higher education.

Twelve

✯✯✯✯✯✯✯✯✯✯✯✯✯✯✯

BRIEFLY REVIEWED

✯✯✯✯✯✯✯✯✯✯✯✯✯✯✯

The books listed here could probably be classified elsewhere. But time did not allow reading more of them and hence they are cited for the most part without comment. However, they have all been examined and included because of clear significance for higher education. An equal or greater number were received but not included because to have done so would have strained this reviewer's already loose definition of higher education.

John Andes
A Systems Approach to University Organization
Gainesville, Fla.: Institute of Higher Education, 1970

Briefly Reviewed

Howard S. Becker (Ed.)
Campus Power Struggle
Chicago: Aldine, 1970

This contains a number of essays dealing with campus tensions which had appeared in the magazine *Trans-action*. In general, the point of view of the various authors seems relatively consistent, as exemplified by a paragraph in the editor's introduction:

> *Even those most critical of student movements can see the difficulties and inequities in existing arrangements. But why, many ask, do they have to be so violent about it? Why can't they play by the rules of the game we have always found workable? We can approach this in at least two ways. We can question the viability of a system in which some people never win. We can also suggest that the matters at issue involve fundamental status realignments that those in power will not willingly contemplate; changes that can prevent becoming issues under the existing rules of the game.*

Ronald C. Benge
Libraries and Cultural Change
Hamden, Conn.: Archon, 1970

Allen E. Beyer
College and University Faculty: A Statistical Description
Washington, D.C.: American Council on Education, 1970

John G. Bolin and Tom McMurrain
Student-Faculty Ratios in Higher Education
Athens, Ga.: Institute of Higher Education, 1970

The Literature of Higher Education 1971

Irene A. Braden
The Undergraduate Library
Chicago: American Library Association, 1970

Theodore Brameld
The Climactic Decades: Mandate to Education
New York: Praeger, 1970

John S. Brubacher
The Courts and Higher Education
San Francisco: Jossey-Bass, 1970

Gene A. Budig (Ed.)
Perceptions in Public Higher Education
Lincoln, Neb.: University of Nebraska Press, 1970

The essays deal generally with the various categories of administration and were prepared in the context of a single institution.

John Cameron
The Development of Education in East Africa
New York: Institute of International Studies, Teachers College, Columbia University, 1970

M. M. Chambers
Above High School
Danville, Ill.: Interstate, 1970

Briefly Reviewed

The College Graduate: His Early Employment and Job Satisfaction
Chicago: College Placement Council, 1970

J. A. Corry
Farewell the Ivory Tower: Universities in Transition
Montreal: McGill-Queens University Press, 1970

These are collected addresses of J. A. Corry, who was principal of Queens University from 1961 to 1968.

William R. Corson
Promise or Peril: The Black College Student in America
New York: Norton, 1970

William L. Deegan and Kenneth P. Mortimer
Faculty in Governance at the University of Minnesota
Berkeley: Center for Research and Development in Higher Education, 1970

Effective Use of Resources in State Higher Education
Atlanta, Ga.: Southern Region Education Board, 1970

Frank L. Ellsworth and Martha A. Burns
Student Activism in American Higher Education
Washington, D.C.: American College Personnel Association, 1970

The Literature of Higher Education 1971

The Embattled University
Daedalus, Winter 1970

John H. Fenton and Gail Gleason
Student Power at the University of Massachusetts: A Case Study
Amherst, Mass.: University of Massachusetts, Bureau of Government Research, 1969

Ben C. Fisher
Duties and Responsibilities of University Trustees
Raleigh, N.C.: North Carolina Board of Higher Education, 1969

Walter Gellhorn and R. Kent Greenawalt
The Sectarian College and the Public Purse. Fordham: A Case Study
Dobbs Ferry, N.Y.: Oceania, 1970

This reports a study commissioned by Fordham University to help the institution make judgments about its educational and legal posture. It is written in the context of a general awareness that privately supported institutions are in serious trouble; many believe that unless public support can be forthcoming, private institutions are likely to go under. It was to seek ways of obtaining public funds for a sectarian institution that the study was commissioned. The authors seem generally skeptical that great public support for parochial institutions will be forthcoming. But they also see using the Fordham example to show how institutions can reform themselves and stay economically viable.

Briefly Reviewed

Angelo C. Gillie
Post Secondary Occupational Education: An Overview and Strategies
University Park, Md.: Center for the Study of Higher Education, 1970

Judith Groch
The Right to Create
Boston: Little, Brown, 1970

David A. Hamburg
Psychiatry as a Behavioral Science
Englewood Cliffs, N.J.: Prentice-Hall, 1970

Irvin L. Harlacher
The Community Dimension of the Community College
Englewood Cliffs, N.J.: Prentice-Hall, 1970

Based on the administrative experience and visits to thirty-seven community colleges, the book describes and makes some attempt to analyze how junior colleges relate to communities and how they mount community service programs.

Herman Edward Harms
The Concept of in Loco Parentis in Higher Education
Gainesville, Fla.: Institute of Higher Education, 1970

John W. Harris (Ed.)
The American University: Some Dilemmas and Alternatives
Athens, Ga.: University of Georgia, 1970

The Literature of Higher Education 1971

Ann M. Heiss
Challenges to Graduate Schools
San Francisco: Jossey-Bass, 1970

Higher Education and the Nation's Health
New York: McGraw-Hill, 1970

Harold L. Hodgkinson and Myron B. Bloy, Jr. (Eds.)
Identity Crisis in Higher Education
San Francisco: Jossey-Bass, 1970

Harold L. Hodgkinson and L. Richard Meeth (Eds.)
Power and Authority: Transformation of Campus Governance
San Francisco: Jossey-Bass, 1970

Stanley O. Ikenberry
A Profile of Proliferating Institutes: A Study of Selected Characteristics of Institutes and Centers in Fifty-One Land Grant Institutions
University Park, Md.: Center for the Study of Higher Education, 1970

H. Leonard Jondahl
Unrest on the Campus
New York: Friendship Press, 1970

Charles B. Johnson and William G. Katzenmeyer
Management Information Systems in Higher Education: The State of the Art
Durham, N.C.: Duke University Press, 1969

Briefly Reviewed

This is a paperback, offset-printed report of a conference held at Duke in 1969 where papers were given on a number of ESSO Education Foundation-supported attempts at applying new management techniques to colleges and universities. Some of the projects have been completed but several were still in process. As a status document this is excellent but it is far from a definitive treatment in such a new and rapidly growing field.

Julius R. Krevans and Peter J. Condliffe
Reform of Medical Education: The Effect of Student Unrest
Washington, D.C.: National Academy of Sciences, 1970

Ben Lawrence et al.
Outputs of Higher Education: Their Identification, Measurement and Evaluation
Boulder, Colo.: Western Interstate Commission on Higher Education, July 1970

Less Time, More Options
New York: McGraw-Hill, 1970

The Making of Modern Science by Graphical Studies
Daedalus, Fall 1970

Barrett John Mandel
Literature and the English Department
Champaign, Ill.: National Council of Teachers of English, 1970

The Literature of Higher Education 1971

This is one professor's appeal for a reevaluation of the goals and methods in college English departments and courses. The author desires to make the study of literature into the stimulating, meaningful experience it should be.

William James McKeefery
Parameters of Learning
Carbondale, Ill.: Southern Illinois University Press, 1970

Redford G. Moon, Jr.
National Planning for Education
New York: The Academy for Educational Development, 1970

Arnold S. Nash
The Choice Before the Humanities
Durham, N.C.: Regional Education Laboratory for the Carolinas and Virginia, 1970

These are papers delivered at a conference which explored to what extent the insights of the humanities are needed to supplement the findings of the social sciences in any adequate attempt to understand an institution of higher learning. Some of the articles were commissioned and some found existent in the literature.

The Open Door Colleges
New York: McGraw-Hill, 1970

Ernest C. Palola
The Sociology of Planning
Berkeley: Center for Research and Development in Higher Education, 1970

Briefly Reviewed

Robert J. Parden
An Introduction to Program Planning, Budgeting and Evaluation for Universities
Santa Clara, Calif.: University of Santa Clara, Office of Institutional Planning, 1970

William G. Perry, Jr.
Forms of Intellectual and Ethical Development in the College Years
New York: Holt, Rinehart & Winston, 1970

An interpretation based on in-depth interviews with students reflecting on what has contributed to their own personal development. Shorter than Katz' *No Time for Youth,* it uses similar sorts of data.

Proceedings of Symposium on Education and Federal Laboratory University Relationships
New York: Arno Press, 1970

Report of the Commission on Tests
New York: College Entrance Examination Board, 1970

ROTC Programs at State Colleges and Universities
Washington, D.C.: American Association of State Colleges and Universities, 1969

Salaries in Higher Education 1970
Washington, D.C.: National Education Association, 1970

The Literature of Higher Education 1971

Erwin T. Sanders and Jennifer G. Ward
Bridges to Understanding
New York: McGraw-Hill, 1970

Michael I. Schafer
Student Role of Teachers: Faculty Development in the Community College
Gainesville, Fla.: Institute of Higher Education, 1970

Robert E. Sharer
There Are No Islands: The Concerns and Potentials of Continuing Education
North Quincy, Mass.: Christopher, 1970

Gabriel Solomon and Richard E. Snow
Commentaries on Research in Instructional Media: An Examination of Conceptual Schemes
Bloomington, Ind.: School of Education, Indiana University, 1970

The Student Newspaper: Report of the Special Commission on the Student Press to the President of the University of California
Washington, D.C.: American Council on Education, 1970

The Trustee: Key to Progress in the Small College
Washington, D.C.: Council for the Advancement of Small Colleges, 1970

Conference proceedings.

Briefly Reviewed

The Two-Year College and Its Students: An Empirical Report
Iowa City, Iowa: American College Testing Program, 1970

Stanley P. Wagner
The End of Revolution
Cranbury, N.J.: A. S. Barnes, 1970

Robert C. Ward
Mr. President, the Decision Is Yours
Lexington, Ky.: College of Education, University of Kentucky, 1969

Warren W. Willingham
Professional Development of Financial Aid Officers
New York: College Entrance Examination Board, 1970

D. Parker Young
The Law and Student Protest
Athens, Ga.: University of Georgia, 1970

Conference proceedings.

D. Parker Young
The Legal Aspects of Student Dissent and Discipline in Higher Education
Athens, Ga.: Institute of Higher Education, 1970

D. Parker Young and Donald D. Gehring
Briefs of Selected Court Cases Affecting Student Dissent and Discipline in Higher Education
Athens, Ga.: Institute of Higher Education, 1970

INDEX OF TITLES AND AUTHORS

A

AAUP Handbook on Academic Freedom and Tenure, 15
Abstract for Action, An, 127
Academia in Anarchy, 35
Academic Deanship in American Colleges and Universities, 9
Academic Degree Structures, 47
Academic Revolution, The, 8
Academic Values and Mass Education, 101

Academics on the Line, 69
Agony and Promise, 18
AIKEN, H. D., 25
Alienated Student, The, 77
Alternative to Irrelevance, 30
American College, The, 18
American College and American Culture, The, 55
American Junior Colleges, 28
American Personality and the Creative Arts, 129

Index

American Universities and Colleges, 28
American University, The, 6
ANDES, J., 144
Annual Guides to Graduate Study, 25
ARON, R., 17
Arrogance on Campus, 88
Arts on Campus, The, 128
ASTIN, A., 16, 18
ASTIN, H. S., 137
Autonomy of Public Colleges, The, 11
AXEN, R., 80

B

BARZUN, J., 6
BASKIN, S., 22
BAYER, A. E., 137
BECKER, H. S., 145
BELL, D., 19, 26
Benefits, Cost and Finance of Public Higher Education, 139
BENGE, R. C., 145
BERELSON, B., 24
BERG, I., 133
BEYER, A. E., 145
Black College, The, 24
Black Power and Student Rebellion, 23
Black Studies in the University, 24
BLACKWELL, T., 13
BLOCKER, C., 29
BLOY, M. B., JR., 150
BLUM, R. H., 17
BOALT, G., 133
BOLIN, J. G., 145
BOWEN, H., 8
BRADEN, I. A., 146
BRAMELD, T., 146
BROWN, J. D., 9
BRUBACHER, J. S., 146
BUCHANAN, J. M., 35
BUDIG, G. A., 146
BURNS, G. P., 12
BURNS, M. A., 147
BURRIN, F. K., 52
BUTZ, O., 16

By Any Means Necessary, 80
BYSE, C., 13

C

CALIFANO, J. A., JR., 67
CAMERON, J., 146
Campus Apocalypse, 18
Campus Crisis, The, 76
Campus in the Modern World, The, 110
CAREY, J. T., 17
CARMICHAEL, O., 66
Catholic Education in a Changing World, 22
Catholic University, 100
Century of Law at Notre Dame, A, 61
Challenge and Perspective in Higher Education, 87
CHAMBERS, M. M., 13–14, 37, 146
Change in Educational Policy, 43
Changing Dimensions in International Education, 112
Changing Values in College, 18
CHICKERING, A. W., 26
Church, the University, and Social Policy, The, 142
CLARK, B. R., 93
Cluster College, The, 96
COHEN, J., 20
College and University Curriculum, 20
College Curriculum and Student Protest, 20
College Dropout and the Utilization of Talent, The, 16
College Drug Scene, The, 17
College Graduate, The, 147
College Health Services in the United States, 27
College Presidency, The, 90
College Student Personnel, 116
Colleges of the Forgotten Americans, 95
Commission on the Government of the University of Toronto, 37

Index

Comprehensive Junior College Curriculum, The, 130
Computer in American Education, The, 14
CONDLIFFE, P. J., 151
Conflict of Generations, The, 16
Conformity, 23, 30
Confrontation, 26
Confrontations, 74
CONNERY, R. H., 135
Contemporary College Students and the Curriculum, 20
Contemporary Critics of Education, 61
COOMBS, P. H., 21
CORRY, J. A., 147
CORSON, W. R., 147
COUNELIS, J. S., 124
Counseling of College Students, The, 27
Creative College Student, The, 16
Culture of the University, 9
Current Campus Issues, 107

D

Daedalus, 2, 107, 148, 151
DANIELS, A. K., 69
DAVIS, J. A., 131
DEEGAN, W. L., 38, 147
DE GRAF, L. B., 61
DEVLETOGOLU, N. E., 35
Dialogue with Erik Erikson, 26
DIBDEN, A., 9
Distinctive College, The, 93
DRESSEL, P. L., 9, 20, 35, 39
Drugs on the College Campus, 17
DUNHAM, E. A., 95
Dynamics of Academic Reform, 23

E

EBLE, K. B., 116
Education and Employment, 140
Education and Identity, 26
Education and Jobs, 133
Education and the Barricades, 15
Education and the Idea of Mankind, 25

Education for National Development, 21
Edward Charles Elliott, Educator, 52
Effective College Teaching, 120
Effective Use of Resources in State Higher Education, 147
Efficiency of Freedom, The, 11
EHRENREICH, B., 17
EHRENREICH, J., 17
EICHEL, L. E., 70
ELAM, S., 41
ELLSWORTH, F. L., 147
Elusive Revolution, The, 17
Embattled University, The, 148
Emergence of the American University, The, 8
EMMERSON, D. K., 17
Employment Relations in Higher Education, 41
EULAU, H., 35, 41
EVANS, R. I., 26
Experiment at Berkeley, 20

F

Faculty Advising in Colleges and Universities, 27, 118
FELDMAN, K. A., 18
FENTON, J. H., 148
FEUER, L., 16
FISHER, B. C., 148
FITZGERALD, L. E., 116
Five Counter Revolutionists in Higher Education, 56
FOLGER, J. K., 137
FOOTE, C., 9
FOSTER, J., 68
FRANKEL, C., 8, 15, 26
Free Access to Higher Education, 50
Freedom and Repression in Higher Education, 14
FREEMAN, R., 8
From Backwater to Mainstream, 97
FUNK, R., 13

G

GAFF, J. G., 96
GAMSON, Z., 101

Index

GARDNER, J., 19
GEHRING, D. D., 156
GEIGER, L. G., 53
GELLHORN, W., 148
General Education in School and College, 66
GILLIE, A. C., 149
GLEASON, G., 148
GLEAZER, E. J., JR., 28
GLENNAN, T. K., 21
GLENNY, L., 11
GOHEEN, R. F., 83
GOLLIN, A. E., 21
GOULD, S. E., 32, 84
Graduate and Professional Education, 127
Graduate Education in the United States, 24
Graduate Education Today, 24, 66
GREELEY, A. M., 18, 22, 97, 103
GREEN, T. F., 25
GREENAWALT, R. K., 148
GREENE, G., 17
Grim Generation, The, 73
GROCH, J., 149
Guide to Graduate Study—Programs Leading to the Ph.D., 25
Guidelines for Jesuit Higher Education, 5
GUSFIELD, J., 101

H

HABER, D., 20
HAMBURG, D. A., 149
Handbook for Trustees, 49
Handbook of College and University Administration, 43
HANDLIN, M. F., 55
HANDLIN, O., 55
HANSEN, W. L., 139
HARCLEROAD, F. F., 108
HARDEE, M. D., 118
HARLACHER, I. C., 149
HARMS, H. E., 149
HARRIS, J., 71
HARRIS, J. W., 149
HARRIS, M. R., 56

HARRIS, S., 11
Harvard, 73
Harvard Strike, The, 70
HAYDEN, T., 16
HEFFERLIN, JB L., 23, 42
HEGENER, K. C., 25
HEISS, A. M., 150
HEIST, P., 16
HENDERSON, A. D., 86
Higher Education and the Nation's Health, 150
Higher Education: Demand and Response, 110
Higher Education: Dimensions and Directions, 112
Higher Education in the Age of Science, 91
Higher Education in the Fifty States, 37
Higher Education: Resources and Finance, 11
Higher Education: Some New Developments, 22
HILBERRY, C., 29
HODGKINSON, H. L., 98, 150
HOPPE, W. A., 99
HORN, F. H., 87
Howard University: The First Hundred Years, 1867–1967, 60
Human Nature of a University, The, 83
Human Resources and Higher Education, 137
Humanities Today, The, 125
HUTCHINS, R. M., 25

I

IKENBERRY, S. O., 150
Impact of College on Students, The, 18
Information Services for Academic Administration, 42
INGRAM, M., 14
Innovative Spirit, The, 86
Institutions in Transition, 98
Investment in Innovation, 65

Index

Islands of Innovation Expanding, 22
Issues of the Seventies, 108

J

JACOB, P., 18
JENCKS, C., 8
JOHNSON, B. L., 22
JOHNSON, C. B., 4, 151
JOHNSON, F. C., 39
JOHNSON, W. F., 116
Joint Participation and Decision Making, 38
JONDAHL, H. L., 150

K

KAHN, E. J., JR., 73
KAHN-HUT, R., 69
KATZ, J., 26
KATZENMEYER, W. G., 4, 151
KAVANAUGH, R., 73
KEETON, M., 29
KELLY, W., 119
KENISTON, K., 16
KENNAN, G., 8, 16
KERR, C., 6, 39, 69
Knowledge and the Future of Man, 25
KNOWLES, A. S., 43
KNOWLES, J. H., 20
KOERNER, J., 57
KORN, H. A., 78
KREVANS, J. R., 151
KRISTOL, I., 26
KUNEN, J. S., 16

L

LADD, D. R., 43
LANTZ, H., 133
LAW, D., 68
LAWRENCE, B., 151
Leaders, Teachers, and Learners in Academe, 109
LEHRER, S., 109
LEIBERMAN, M., 41
LE MELLE, T. J., 24
LE MELLE, W. J., 24
LESLIE, W., 119

LEVI, A. W., 125
LEVI, E. H., 88
Liberal University, The, 9
Librarian Speaking, The, 118
LIGON, J. F., 74
LOCKMILLER, D. A., 59
LOGAN, R. W., 60
Long March, Short Spring, 17
LYLE, G. R., 118
LYSAUGHT, J. P., 127

M

MC CLUSKEY, N. G., 100
MC CONNELL, T. R., 15, 38
MC EVOY, J., 23
MC GRATH, E. J., 45
MC KEEFERY, W. J., 152
MC MURRAIN, T., 145
MAHONEY, M., 128
MANDEL, B. J., 151
MARCUS, P. M., 39
MARGOLIS, J. D., 110
MARMION, H., 41
MARTIN, W. B., 23, 30
MAYHEW, L. B., 20, 88, 127
MEETH, L. R., 150
METZGER, W., 15
MICKELSON, J. C., 129
MILLER, A., 23
MILLER, S. J., 121
MILLS, O., 76
Mirror of Brass, The, 14
MOON, R. G., JR., 152
MORTIMER, K. P., 38, 147
MOSKOW, M. H., 41
Mr. President, The Decision Is Yours. Deal Out the Dough, 48, 155

N

NASH, A. S., 152
NEWCOMB, T. M., 18
NIBLETT, W. R., 110
NICHOLS, D. C., 75–76
No Time for Youth, 26
NORRIS, W., 116
NOSOW, S., 46
NOWLIS, H. H., 17

Index

O

OETINGER, A. G., 122
ONG, W. J., 25
ORLANS, H., 28
OSMAN, H., 61
Outward Fringe, The, 14

P

PALOLA, E. C., 152
PARDEN, R. J., 153
Parsons College Bubble, 57
PAULSEN, F. R., 112
PENTONY, D., 80
People in Context, 104
Perceptions in Higher Education, 146
PERKINS, J., 13
PERRY, W. G., JR., 153
Perspectives on Campus Tensions, 75
PERVIN, L. A., 16
PHILLIPS, E. L., JR., 42
Point of View, 88
Police on Campus, 16
Policies and Practices in Evening Colleges, 1969, 99
POTTER, P., 16
Prescription for Leadership, 121
Problems and Prospects in International Education, 21
Proceedings of Symposium on Education and Federal Laboratory University Relations, 153
Professional School and World Affairs, The, 21
Professional Self Images and Organization Orientations of a General Education Faculty, 46
Protest: Student Activism in America, 61, 68

Q

QUICK, R., 25
QUINLEY, H., 41

R

RAUH, M. A., 50
Recent Alumni and Higher Education, 103
Recognition and Evaluation of Teaching, The, 116
Reflections on Big Science, 28
Reforming of General Education, The, 19, 26
REINERT, P. C., 89
Relevant Professor, The, 92
Report of the Commission on Tests, 153
REYNOLDS, J. W., 130
RIESMAN, D., 8, 101
Right to Say We, The, 81
Rights and Responsibilities, 107
RIKER, H., 27
RITCHIE, M. A. F., 90
ROBINSON, A. L., 24
ROGAN, D. L., 18
ROGERS, W. R., 77
ROTC Programs at State Colleges and Universities, 153
Run, Computer, Run, 122

S

Salaries in Higher Education 1970, 153
SALEM, J. M., 123
SAMPSON, E. E., 78
SANDERS, E. T., 154
SANFORD, N., 18, 25
SAVIO, M., 16
SCANLON, D. G., 21
SCHAFER, M. I., 154
Scholars on Parade, 59
SCHWAB, J., 20
Science Policy and the University, 28
Secularization and the University, 22
SERVIN, M. P., 62
SHARER, R. E., 154
SHARP, L. M., 140
Should Students Share the Power?, 45
SHUSTER, G. N., 22
SIEGEL, M., 27
SINGLETARY, O. A., 28
B. F. Skinner: The Man and His Ideas, 26
SMALL, S. A., 91

161

Index

SMELSER, N. J., 131
SMITH, G. K., 18, 63, 113
SMITH, H. E., 22
SMITH, R., 80
SNOW, R. E., 154
Sociology, 131
SOLOMON, G., 154
Southern California and Its University: A History of U.S.C. 1880–1964, 62
SPEATH, J. L., 103
Sponsored Research in American Universities and Colleges, 28
SPURR, S. H., 47
State Officials and Higher Education, 41
STERN, G. G., 104
STRAIN, R. E., 92
STRICKLAND, S., 28
STROUP, H., 27
Struggle and Promise: A Future for Colleges, 29
Student Activism and Protest, 78
Student Newspaper, 154
Student Revolution, 67
Students and Politics in Developing Nations, 17
Students in Revolt, 71
Students Without Teachers, 6
STULL, H., 38

T

TAYLOR, H., 6, 16, 25–26
Teacher as a Writer, The, 123
Teacher Education Reappraisal, 66
Teaching in the American Junior College, 119
TICKTON, S., 13
To Be a Phoenix, 124
To Make a Difference, 16
Today's Academic Condition, 84
Toward a Philosophy of Organized Student Activities, 27
Toward Community in University Government, 37
Troubled Campus, The, 113

Trustee, The, 154
Trustees in Higher Education, 12
TUSSMAN, J., 20
Twenty-Five Years: 1945–1970, 63
Two-Year College, The, 29
Two-Year College and Its Students, The, 16, 155

U

ULICH, R., 25
Uncommitted, The, 16
UNDERWOOD, K., 142
Universities and Research, 133
University Development, Continuity and Change, 114
University in Turmoil, 26
Urban Catholic University, The, 89
Uses of the University, The, 6

V

VEYSEY, L. R., 8
Views of Medical Education and Medical Care, 20
Voluntary Accreditation, 53

W

WAGNER, S. P., 155
WALLER, W., 26
WALLERSTEIN, I., 26
WALTERS, E., 24
WARD, J. G., 154
WARD, R. C., 48, 155
WEINBERG, A., 28
WEISBROD, B. E., 139
WICKE, M. F., 49
WILLIAMSON, E. G., 27
WILLINGHAM, W. W., 3, 35, 50, 155
WILSON, I. H., 62
WOODRING, P., 65
World Educational Crisis, The, 21

Y

YOUNG, D. P., 155–156
Young Radicals, The, 16

Z

ZORZA, R., 81